Sports Law in Russia

Sports Law in Russia

Second Edition

Olga Rymkevich

This book was originally published as a monograph in the International Encyclopaedia of Laws/Sports Law.

Founding Editor: Roger Blanpain
General Editor: Frank Hendrickx
Volume Editor: Michele Colucci

Wolters Kluwer

Published by:
Kluwer Law International B.V.
PO Box 316
2400 AH Alphen aan den Rijn
The Netherlands
E-mail: international-sales@wolterskluwer.com
Website: lrus.wolterskluwer.com

Sold and distributed in North, Central and South America by:
Wolters Kluwer Legal & Regulatory U.S.
7201 McKinney Circle
Frederick, MD 21704
United States of America
Email: customer.service@wolterskluwer.com

Sold and distributed in all other countries by:
Air Business Subscriptions
Rockwood House
Haywards Heath
West Sussex
RH16 3DH
United Kingdom
Email: international-customerservice@wolterskluwer.com

ISBN 978-94-035-0053-9

e-Book: ISBN 978-94-035-0054-6
web-PDF: ISBN 978-94-035-0055-3

The Author

Olga Rymkevich is a senior researcher in labour law and industrial relations at the Marco Biagi Foundation, University of Modena and Reggio Emilia, Modena (Italy). She graduated in St. Petersburg State University, Russia in foreign languages and international relations and in Economics in the University of Modena, Italy and Reggio Emilia and has a degree of PhD in Labour Law (University of St. Petersburg, Russia). Her research interests include international and comparative labour law with a particular focus on sport law. She collaborates with the Sport Law and Policy Centre (Rome, Italy). She also serves as a managing editor of The International Journal of Comparative Labour Law and Industrial Relations (Kluwer Law International).

The Author

Table of Contents

List of Abbreviations

AC RF	Administrative Code RF
AIBA	International Boxing Association
ANADO	Association of National Anti-Doping Organizations
CAS	Court of Arbitration for Sport
CC RF	Civil Code RF
CIS	Commonwealth of Independent States
FAS	Federal Antimonopoly Service
FIBT	International Bobsleigh and Skeleton Federation
FIDE	World Chess Federation
FIFA	Fédération Internationale de Football Association International Federation of Association Football
FIFPRO	Fédération Internationale des Associations de Footballeurs Professionnels
FMBA	Federal Medico-Biological Agency
FZ	Federal Law
FISA	International Rowing Federation
FUR	Football Union of Russia
IAAF	International Association of Athletics Federation
IBU	International Biathlon Union
IOC	International Olympic Committee
KHL	Kontinental Hockey League
KZoT	(Kodex Zakonov o Trude) Soviet Labour Code (1971)
LC RF	Labour Code RF
Minsport	Ministry of Sport
OCRF	Olympic Committee of the Russian Federation
PC RF	Penal Code RF
	Trade union of workers in the sphere of physical culture, sport and tourism of the RF
RFF	Regional Football Federation
RIHF	Russian Ice Hockey Federation

RUSADA	Russian Anti-Doping Agency
TC RF	Tax Code
UEFA	Union of European Football Associations
UN	United Nations
USSR	Union of Soviet Socialist Republics
VAT	Value Added Tax
WADA	World Anti-Doping Agency
WCIOM	Russian Public Opinion Research Centre

Acknowledgements

I would like to thank the editors, in particular Michele Colucci, Joeri Lauwers and Frank Hendrickx for the useful suggestions. I would like to express a particular gratitude to Dr. Paola Reggiani Gelmini and Prof. Marina Orlandi Biagi for their support of my work and to Prof. William Bromwich for the linguistic assistance. Finally I would like to thank my mother for encouraging me in this work.

1–4

General Introduction

Chapter 1. Introduction

1. It is difficult to overestimate the importance of sport in modern society. It plays a crucial role as a means to promote healthy lifestyle, to create a system of individual and collective values, to help people socialize, to prevent them from adopting harmful habits, to develop a sense of patriotism, solidarity, mutual respect and self-esteem, to promote equal opportunities, etc. An active lifestyle contributes to longevity and better health outcomes resulting in lower public expenditure for the national healthcare system and a reduction in absenteeism from work and compulsory military service. In addition, sport represents an important strategic and economic factor influencing national markets, international relations, tourism, the quality of the labour force and the armed forces. In international relations sport has traditionally served as a means to enhance national prestige and to strengthen international cultural relations. As a social phenomenon sport must be regarded in connection with the economic, social and political context and consequently its legal regulation should constantly keep pace with the latest developments at the international and national level.

2. The case of Russia is emblematic in this regard. Twentieth century was marked by a number of serious turbulences such as the revolution of 1917, collapse of the communist regime in 1991 and successive deep economic crises and transition to the market economy with a relatively short period of prosperity in the beginning of twenty-first century followed from 2009 by the next wave of the world economic crises. Not surprisingly general legal framework, including the sport-related one, did not always keep pace with such rapid changes and some provisions need to be updated.

3. Since the scope of this contribution is to provide mainly the legal analysis of sport regulation in Russia, only a brief historical excursus for the introductory purposes will be hereby provided.

4. In Tsarist Russia sport was a privilege of *elite* and few people, mainly belonging to a noble society, could allow practising it. However in this period for a number of reasons sport received a strong impetus for further development. During the First and the Second World Wars, sport was militarized and such an approach persisted even after the end of the Second World War. During the Cold War mass physical culture and sport was aimed at training people, especially the youth, to keep them prepared to the 'hypothetic' military actions. To pursuit this goal, compulsory sport training was introduced already from the beginning of school and then continued in the technical schools and universities. Quite a wide range of preparation on various kinds of sport was provided including shooting, skiing, dogfight, grenade throwing, swimming and water crossing, etc.[1]

5. During this period sport was 'overloaded' by the Soviet ideology and served as powerful propaganda of the Soviet lifestyle as opposed to the capitalist one. Accordingly it received considerable attention in the national literature, cinema and art in general. Soviet sport was part of the ideology, politics and culture and by studying its representation in works of art one could understand better the history and ideology.[2] Sport champions were treated like national heroes even if formally they were entitled to the same economic treatment and employment conditions like any ordinary Soviet employee.

6. Like all other spheres of life, sport was regulated by the state in a centralized way. Mass sport was actively supported by the USSR government by means of extensive funding and active propaganda.[3] The underlining idea was that sport should be accessible for everyone. Sport competitions at various levels were rather frequent.[4] Mass sport in Soviet period laid foundations for the development of the top-level professional sport.

7. However till 1988 in the USSR professional sport was not specifically regulated.[5] The first step in professionalization of sport was the regulation of the Soviet of Ministers from 2 August 1988 N 945,[6] so formally professional sport in Russia is a still a relatively 'young' phenomenon.

1. So-called GTO (in Russian) norms existed from 1931 to 1991. Abbreviation means: to be ready to labour and defence. These norms were suspended after the *perestroika* and reintroduced again in March 2014 (presidential provision 172-FZ from 24 Feb. 2014). They became active from 1 Sept. 2014 for all schools. GTO includes special sport normatives differentiated by eleven age groups and gender and three marks of distinction: gold, silver and bronze. People who successfully achieved good results in passing GTO complex can count on some material benefits. So the students may increase scholarships and workers may receive bonuses which amount is determined by the employer. Moreover students with excellent GTO results will be facilitated in entrance exams for higher educational institutions. http://www.gto-normy.ru/.
2. M. O'Mahony, *Sport in the USSR. Physical culture- visual culture*, Reaktion books, London 2006 (In Russian). (М. О'Махоуни, *Спорт в СССР, Физическая культура – визуальная культура*, Новое литературное обозрение, перевод с английского Е. Ляминой, А. Фишман, М, 2010). It was paid attention in works of A. Rodchenko, D. Vertov, A. Samohvalov, A. Deyneka, Komar, Melamid, etc.
3. During the existence of USSR there were more than 3,000 stadiums, 60,000 sports halls, 1,300 swimming pools, 0.5 million sport grounds, 100,000 football fields, 18,000 shooting ranges, 7,000 ski lodges; the turnover of sport industry before the Olympic games was around RUB 3 billion. (http://museumsport.ru/wheelofhistory/mass-sports/).
4. Around 300 All-Soviet competitions per year. http://museumsport.ru/wheelofhistory/mass-sports/).
5. T. Y. Korshunova, *The development of legislation on labour of professional sportsmen*, Labour law, N. 5, 2006 (in Russian) (Т. Ю. Коршунова, Развитие законодательства о труде профессиональных спортсменов //Трудовое право, N 5, 2006).
6. The regulation of the Soviet of Ministers of URSS VZSPC (All-Union Central Soviet of Trade Unions) and ZK VLKSM (Central Committee of All-Union Leninist Young Communist League) from 2 Aug. 1988 N 945 'On improvement of the football management and other kinds of sport and additional measures to manage teams and sportsmen in main kinds of sport'.

8. The end of the communist regime and the transition to the market economy were accompanied by the far-reaching reforms in all the spheres, including sport. The fall of iron curtain and opening of the frontiers provided a wide range of new opportunities but at the same time put forward new challenges.

9. Nowadays like in many other countries sport in Russia has been progressively commercialized becoming a source of extremely high economic revenues. Moreover after the passage to the market economy and abandoning of 'collectivism',[7] more individualistic approach to sport has been developed. Now people consider it not only a source of income or entertainment but also see in it a long-term personal investment as in a modern society a considerable number of jobs require 'a smart image' and medical services after the large-scale privatization are becoming increasingly expensive.

10. From the financial perspective after the collapse of the USSR many problems have arisen due to the lack of funding. With privatization the funds for the reconstruction of the obsolete sport infrastructures and sportsmen training were considerably reduced. Moreover because of the lack of the appropriate legal regulation and transparency the incomes from the sport lotteries and other sport-related commercial undertakings did not flow to the federal budget. As a consequence even if sport federations became independent in practice they did not have sufficient economic resources and often could barely sustain their costs. Sport services became expensive and many talented people went abroad in search of better carrier opportunities. Also mass sport lost its significance as it became expensive for major part of the people. The negative consequences were felt almost immediately. In fact the period of early 1990s was marked by high rate of criminality, harmful substances abuse, low birth and high mortality rate.

11. In the beginning of twenty-first century a number of active steps were undertaken with the aim of improving legal regulation of sport in order to ensure better economic conditions for sportsmen and provide more legal certainty for sport clubs and other sport stakeholders. Albeit an undoubted progress there is still a need to eliminate some gaps and collisions between the national norms belonging to other branches of law and sport law norms as well as to ensure better compliance of national legal norms with the international standards.

12. Both emblematic and controversial in this regard are special laws adopted in relation to the preparation of the Sochi 2014 Olympic games (Federal Law 310-FZ from 1.12.2007, known as 'Olympic Law'), which introduced a lot of facilitations for the organizers in matter of fiscal, administrative, civil, immigration and labour law for the period of the Olympics as well as Federal Law 7.07.2013 N 108-FZ On organization of International Federation of Association Football (FIFA) World Cup Russia 2018 (hereinafter Football law), which will be better examined in the following sections.

13. Due to the broad nature of the topic, in analysing the current state of art in the sphere of sport in Russia, this paper will focus mainly on regulation of professional football, that is self-evidently a domain of the significant economic and social importance even though the other kinds of sport as well as relevant sport-related issues will be highlighted where necessary.

---

7. Important cultural feature of the Soviet period.

14. From the beginning of the twenty-first century the funding of the mass physical culture and sport has increased together with the improvement of the general financial situation of Russian people. Healthy lifestyle was actively promoted as a means to improve personal attractiveness. Not occasionally sport includes a large part of the beauty and entertainment industry accounting to the billionaire turnover. On the whole the number of people practising sport has increased as well as the number and quality of the respective sport infrastructures. However a structural change of sport preferences has taken place. The number of people practising fitness increased from 31% (2006) to 43% (2013). This provoked decrease of people practising other kinds of sport like football, basketball, volley, ice hockey, etc., even if the overall number of spectators and fans has even increased.

15. According to the recent statistics of WCIOM,[8] the number of Russians who practise sport increased amounting to 52% in 2013. Over the recent seven years the quota of people practising sport has progressively increased from 6% to 10%. Among those people the quota of people practising sport regularly several times a week increased from 8% to 14%. About 9% of people practise sport once a week, 7% – several times a week, 11% – several times a year. The mostly preferred kinds of sport include complex sport activity (43%), light athletics (15%), swimming (14%), physiotherapy (14%). Less popular kinds of sport are considered football (8%)[9], volley (6%), fighting and basketball (both around 2%) and hockey (1%).[10]

16. Among the reasons to ignore practising sport the Russians claim the lack of time (37%), no need (28%), bad health conditions (23%) and a lack of willpower (22%). Less claimed factors are: lack of financial resources (6%), underdeveloped sporting infrastructure in place of residence (4%), lack of possibility to have personal coach/instructor (3%). There are no exact data of corporate sport activities i.e., how many enterprises create internal sport infrastructures or provide their employees and their families with the free subscriptions to the sport clubs or organize corporate competitions. However recent legislative novelties should stimulate the increase of people practising sport as from 2015 the employer should compensate the employees sport activity and the proportion of these expenses in relation to the total expenses of the enterprise should amount to approximately 0.2%. In particular these measures will include:

8. Russian public opinion research centre, http://www.wciom.com/index.php, the data relate to the survey of 30–31 Mar. 2013 including 1600 respondents from 42 different regions (estimated statistical error – around 3–4%). The other sources regarding general number of people practising sport are less optimistic. So, according to the authors of the strategy of the development of the Russian physical culture and sport till 2020 (http://www.infosport.ru/strategiya/index.html) there are only around 8% of actively economic people systematically practising sport.
9. The Strategy of football development 2020 provides the figure of 2.4 million people who currently practice football in Russia which has increased from 2005, when it was only 1.4 million.
10. http://www.wciom.com/index.php.

- Compensation of the employees practising sport in sport clubs and sections.
- Organization of physical culture and sport measures including those related to GTO norms and compensation of coaches and methodists engaged in realization of such measures.
- Organization of physical culture and health promotion events.
- Acquisition, renovation and maintenance of sport inventory.
- Establishment of new or reconstruction of the existing premises for sport practice.
- Creation of sport clubs at the work place, etc.[11]

17. Currently there are around 14,000 sports clubs in Russia[12] and 238,000 sport infrastructures.[13]

The strategy of the development of physical culture and sport in Russia till 2020[14] as one of priority strategic goals contemplates the increment of the share of people systematically practising sport from 15.9% in 2008, up to 30% in 2015 and up to 40% in 2020.

11. Addendum to the regulation of the Ministry of Labour and Social Protection of the RF from 16 Jun 2014 N 375н introducing amendments in the model list of the annual measures carried out by the employer to improve the employment conditions and reduce professional risks adopted by the regulation of the Ministry of Health and Social Development of the RF on 1 Mar. 2012 N 181 H. However this regulation is not very rigid and many aspects are left to the bargaining of the parties.
12. As compared to 270500 in Austria, http://www.infosport.ru/strategiya/index.html.
13. http://www.wciom.com/index.php.
14. Provision of the RF government from 07 Aug. 2009 N. 1101-p 'On the adoption of the Strategy of the development of physical culture and sport in the RF till 2020'.

Chapter 3. Institutions

18. Among the main institutions in the sport sphere in Russia there is a Ministry of Sport of the Russian Federation, created according to the governmental Decree from 21 May 2012 which transformed the then Ministry of Sport, Tourism and Youth Policy in the current Ministry of Sport.[15]

19. The Ministry of Sport of the RF (hereinafter Minsport RF) is a federal executive body charged with the objectives of the elaboration and carrying out the state sport policy including control and surveillance functions. The ministry acts in observance of the Constitution of the Russian Federation and other federal laws and international treaties. It collaborates with other federal bodies of the subjects of the Russian Federation, local executive bodies and other public organizations at various levels.

20. Another important body is the Olympic Committee of the Russian Federation (OCRF)[16] set up on 1 December 1989. It represents the All-Russian Federation of public associations, voluntary, non-governmental, non-commercial organizations, recognized by the International Olympic Committee (IOC). Its activity is regulated by the laws of the Russian Federation and the Olympic Charter (last updated 9 September 2013) of the IOC. It governs the Olympic movement in Russia, elaborates and conducts general policy for high-level competitive sports in collaboration with the federal executive body reflecting the interests of federations and sportsmen and women.

21. According to the Statute the OCRF was set up for the following purposes:

– to develop and defend the Olympic movement in Russia according to the Olympic Charter;
– to promote Olympic, physical and spiritual education in Russia;
– to enhance the prestige of Russian sport in the international arena;
– to promote participation in sport and top-level professional sports in All-Russian regions.

22. The tasks of the OCRF are:

– to raise awareness among Russians of the main Olympic principles;
– to disseminate knowledge on the Olympic spirit, Olympic movement and Olympic games in educational institutions;
– to assist educational establishments whose activity is linked to the Olympic movement;
– to support Olympic academies, museums and cultural programmes linked to the Olympic movement;
– to defend the interests of sportsmen and women and coaches, sports referees and sports veterans;
– to set up funds and charitable organizations promoting mass sport;

15. The functions in the sphere of tourism were transferred to the Ministry of Culture of the Russian Federation and the functions of youth policy to the Ministry of Education and Science of RF..
16. http://www.olympic.ru/.

- to organize scientific conferences in the field of sport;
- to take action against doping.

23. Article 11 of the Federal Law of the RF of 4 December 2007, 329-FZ 'On Sport in the Russian Federation' (hereinafter: *the Law on Sport*) is devoted to the Olympic movement and the Olympic Committee. According to Article 11(1), the Olympic movement in Russia is part of the international Olympic movement whose aim is to uphold and implement the principles of the Olympic movement, to promote physical culture, to reinforce international sports collaboration and participation in the Olympic games and other sport events under the patronage of the IOC. Moreover, the Olympic Committee defends the rights of the IOC with regard to the use of the Olympic symbols, motto, hymn and flags with exclusive rights in this respect. It fulfils these tasks from its own funding sources, voluntary contributions and the federal budget.[17] In addition it represents Olympic movement in Russia and members of the OCRF in the federal and municipal governmental bodies, Russian and international sport organizations. It approves the composition of national Olympic teams, sends them to participate in the Olympic games and other important international sport events under the aegis of the IOC, provides sport equipment, stay and insurance of the Olympic delegation of the RF in the sport events organized under the aegis of IOC, determines the city of the RF which can apply to the IOC for the awarding of the right to hold Olympic games, etc. Besides it detains the exclusive rights in relation to the use of its own name and official name 'Olympic team of the RF'. Third parties can use these names and their derivatives with commercial aim only upon the written consent of the OCRF, except the use for informative purposes only or in case they acquired the right to broadcast Olympic games and other important sport events under the aegis of the IOC.

24. Finally the independent All-Russian National Anti-Doping Agency 'RUSADA'[18] was created in January 2008 on the initiative of the Federal Agency for Physical Culture and Sport in compliance with the WADA Code and the UNESCO International Convention against Doping in Sport approved at the UNESCO General Assembly in 19 October 2005 and ratified by the Russian Federation 26 December 2006. According to the WADA requirements RUSADA is responsible for the anti-doping testing, implementation of anti-doping rules, educational programmes, research on doping issues and fight against it, investigation in relation to the violation of anti-doping rules, setting up of independent committees and international cooperation. The main objective of RUSADA's activities is to protect athletes' health and their fundamental right to participate in fair, doping-free sport, the objective clearly stated in RUSADA's logo: 'For health and fairness in sport!'

25. RUSADA's personnel includes 23 doping control officers working full-time and almost 50 doping control officers working in the regions, which provides for more than 20,000 samples collected annually. Doping control officers are annually re-accredited and audited.

17. S. V. Alekseyev, *Sports law in Russia*, Unity Dana, Law and legislation, 2nd edition, Moscow, 2012 (in Russian). (Алексеев С. В., *Спортивное право России*, Юнити Дана, Закон и право, 2 издание, М. 2012), 451-452.
18. http://www.rusada.ru/en.

26. RUSADA develops cooperation with the World Anti-Doping Agency, international anti-doping organizations, national anti-doping organizations and a number of international federations worldwide in the field of educational and doping control programmes.

27. In May 2008 RUSADA was approved by the World Anti-Doping Agency as a national anti-doping agency and included into the official WADA list of anti-doping organizations. In 2009 RUSADA became a member of Association of National Anti-Doping Organizations (ANADO). RUSADA is also a member of Regional Anti-Doping Organization in Eastern Europe. Membership in ANADO and RADO enables RUSADA to develop and make the most of anti-doping cooperation with national anti-doping organizations and international federations worldwide.

Recently RUSADA has signed agreements with International Rowing Federation (FISA), International Biathlon Union (IBU) and International Association of Athletics Federations (IAAF). In line with the agreements RUSADA provides sample collection services within the territory of the Russian Federation.

Chapter 4. Sport Governance: In the Name of Autonomy and Specificity

28. In the absence of a comprehensive legal framework regulating sport (a kind of *lex sportiva*)[19] this domain is governed by the interdisciplinary norms belonging to different branches of law (civil, criminal, tax, administrative and so on). Albeit Russia belongs to the continental legal system a number of disputes among legal experts concern especially the role of civil and labour law in regulating sport. The supporters of civil law, inspired by the Anglo-Saxon system, consider that the specificity of sport cannot be fully accounted for by labour law norms, while other experts argue that it is inappropriate to exclude sportsmen and women from the protections provided by labour law. Considering the need for a differentiated approach for this category of workers and in light of the national legal traditions[20] the Russian legislator has given priority to labour law while leaving the option of concluding contracts under the civil law (mainly in the case of individual sports). Moreover Federal Law from 21 July 2014 N 421-FZ 'On amending separate legislative acts of the Russian Federation' in relation to the adoption of the law 'on special evaluation of employment conditions' directly established the priority of the norms of labour law over the norms of civil law. In the new Article 19.1 LC RF it is indicated that in case of the irremovable contradictions in the court in relation to the nature of the relations arisen between employer and employee on the basis of the civil law contract the priority will be given to labour law.[21] Apart from the clear aim to protect the rights of sportsmen another intention was to reduce possible conflicts between civil and labour law norms.

29. During the Soviet period, sport, especially top-level professional sport, received considerable attention as it was an important means for representing the Soviet Union in the international political arena. In the context of political confrontation between the two superpowers, such as USA and USSR top professional sport was a field of fierce competition. As President Kennedy proclaimed in one of his speeches in 1960, 'all the problems of the world could be solved on the basis of the number of missiles and gold medals'. At that time a considerable amount of money was invested in top-level professional sport.[22]

---

19. The proposals to create a sort of *lex sportiva* definitively recognizing thus the autonomy of sport law is discussed in Russian legal literature *see* A. A. Soloviev, The concept of the Sport Code in Russian Federation, Moscow 2009. (А. А. Соловьёв, Концепция проектаСпортивного кодекса Российской Федерации) (in Russian); On the transnational nature of *lex sportiva see* O. Kirilyuk, *Lex sportiva – the concept of transnational sports law*, Law and life, 8/3, 2013. (О. Кирилюк, *Lex sportiva – концепция транснационального спортивного права* // Закон и жизнь, 8/3, 2013) (in Russian).
20. KzOT (1971) considered sportsmen regular employees subject to standard labour law provisions.
21. O. Shevchenko, *Legal doctrine of labour regulation in professional sport and its realisation in Russia*, Dissertation, Moscow, 2014 (in Russian).(О. А. Шевченко, *Правовая доктрина регулирования труда в сфере профессионального спорта и пути ее реализации в России*, диссертация, Москва, 2014
22. S. V. Alekseev, *Sport law in Russia*, UNITI-DANA, 2005, 49.

30. Both mass and high performance sport were encouraged and supported by the state. After *perestroika* and following economic crisis, investments in sport, as in most other economic sectors, were reduced. The negative consequences were felt immediately. The number of athletes practising sport fell down, and many talented sportsmen and women emigrated in search of better training and employment opportunities. Moreover, the lack of specific sports legislation resulted in many clubs suffering economic losses due to the fact that sportsmen and women tended to leave their clubs at short notice or with none at all, with a liability to pay only minimal compensation. All these factors underlined the need for reform of the existing legal framework.

31. Taking into consideration the fact that sport regulation in Russia is based on a mixed model with a significant role for the state together with self-regulation by professional sports bodies (federations/associations),[23] the provisions regulating sport can be found in different legislative acts. Some of them are laid down in the Russian Constitution, federal laws, acts issued by the subjects of the Russian Federation[24] (federal bodies of RF), regulations adopted by sports federations and associations and the terms and conditions of individual contracts. Aspects such as working hours, night work, holidays and salaries of sportsmen and women can be regulated by collective agreement and local normative measures.

32. According to the general principles of law, lower-level legislative acts may not contradict higher-level ones. Moreover, Article 15(4) of the Russian Constitution establishes the priority of international legislative acts ratified by the RF over national law. The Russian Constitution refers to sport in relation to human rights, in connection with the promotion of a healthy lifestyle and special state-supported programmes in favour of those practising sport (Article 41), and in relation to matters jointly regulated by the federation and the subjects of the RF (Article 72).

33. So the specificity of sport is reflected in the adoption of the specific laws on sport, in the autonomy of sport federations in setting up their own rules by means of internal regulations and in the existence of the special system of sport justice. One of the main legislative sources in the field of sport in the RF is the already mentioned 'Law on Sport' of the Russian Federation[25] repealing the Law of 29 April 1999, 80-FZ 'On Physical Culture and Sport in the Russian Federation'.

34. The 'Law on Sport' deals to a great extent with administrative matters such as the division of powers between the federal state and the subjects of the RF (Articles 6 and 8 respectively) and specify measures to prevent duplication of functions of federal executive bodies. It introduces a new legal person such as sport federation (which may be created at local, regional and All-Russian level) which aim is to promote one or more kinds of sport, ensure their propaganda and carry out sport competitions and training of sportsmen for national teams. Only one All-Russian Federation may be accredited on the RF territory on one kind of sport for a maximum period of four

23. Art. 3 comma 3, Law 329-FZ of 4 Dec. 2007 ('Law on Sport').
24. RF is a federal state and consists of the so-called subjects of Russian Federation (federal bodies) which are currently eighty-five. They are equal in their relations with the federal government and dispose of their own executive and legislative powers. They have their own constitutions (or statutes) and own legislation approved by regional parliaments.
25. Last amendments introduced 26 Jul. 2017.

years (Article 14, 'Law on Sport'). To be qualified as All-Russian Federation, it must conform to certain requisites, one of which is to have among its members duly accredited regional sport federations which carry out their activity on the territory of more than half of the subjects of the RF. Moreover its official name must conform to the requirements established by the Russian legislation in relation to public associations, specify its organizational form (public organization), territorial sphere of activity (All-Russian) and kind(s) of sport for which it was created. Also in case of regional federation the executive body of the RF may accredit only one federation for a one kind of sport. In case there is already All-Russian Federation on this kind of sport, the regional federation concerned must be its member (Article 13(5) 'Law on Sport'). The term of accreditation is maximum four years.

35. Moreover the law regulates mechanisms of their accreditation (both regional and All-Russian) and their juridical status. It introduces new notions such as basic kinds of sport, spectator, sport Steward, volunteers, animals participating in competitions, Olympic delegation, Olympic team of Russia, Paralympic delegation, Paralympic team, programme of sport preparation (training), symbolics of sport (physical culture) event, student sport and student sport league, school sport.

36. Among the other issues the law includes mechanisms of recognition of sport disciplines and All-Russian unified register of sport, All-Russian sport classification, All-Russian plan for sport competitions, etc. It also provides distinction between such notions as 'physical culture initiative', 'sport initiative' and 'sport competition' which is important as in practice they require different regulation in terms of the subjects involved and procedures. A special notion of the official sport competition is introduced.[26]

37. Special chapter is dedicated to the preparation of 'reserve players' i.e., education and training of future sportsmen and the responsible institutions are defined in this regard. Other novelties concern training process, sporting equipment, other sport facilities, food, medical treatment, travels, funding and formation of the national teams.

38. Special attention is reserved to the prevention of unlawful influence on sport results (including briberies to sportsmen, referees, team leaders and other participants, coercive actions, or conspiracy) and respective sanctions and preventive measures to combat this phenomenon have been adopted.[27] Moreover persons directly involved are prohibited to bet on competition results.

39. The Law is not limited to the Olympics but also covers the Paralympics and Deaf Olympic Sports. In other words this law defines more concretely respect to its predecessor (Law regulating sport of 29 April 1999, 80-FZ) the conditions of functioning of sport federations and clubs highlighting however mainly the administrative, business and entertainment aspects of sport. The matters of relationship between the sportsmen, coaches and clubs are delegated to the special chapter of the Labour Code. Many of the issues, including employment rights, are regulated by other legislative acts, corporate norms, collective agreement and individual contracts. In particular, unlike the law of

26. A. N. Borisov, *Commentary* to the Federal Law 'On Physical culture and sport in Russian Federation', Justizinform, 2009 (in Russian). (Борисов А.Н., *Комментарий* к Федеральному закону "О физической культуре и спорте в Российской Федерации" (постатейный), Юстицинформ, 2009).

27. Introduced by the Federal Law from 23 Jul. 2013 N. 198-FZ.

1999, it does not provide a distinction between professional and amateur sportsmen. As it may be seen from the definition provided by the Article 2(22) of the 'Law on Sport' 'sportsman is a natural person who practices a chosen kind of sport and participates in sport competitions'. So in practice it unifies under a generic term 'sportsman' professional, amateur and other people somehow engaged in sport practice. The supporters of a such regulatory approach justify it by the fact that the borderline between professional and amateur sport is unclear as well as the criteria of the determination of a professional status of a sportsman may significantly vary for different kinds of sport and that even in the Olympic Charter the notion of professional sportsman is still absent. However juridical vagueness generated by the absence of commonly accepted definitions and the lack of specific norms may in practice give rise to a series of problems for the courts in terms of necessary powers to adopt proper decisions.

40. In order to fill in the existing legal gaps, including those left by the 'Law on Sport', and recognizing that because of the specific nature of sport linked to the intense physical and psychological effort, short professional career, increased risk of injury and finally the entertainment and commercial aspects of sport, athletes require special legislative regulation compared to other categories of workers, the Federal Law 13-FZ on 28 February 2008 'On the amendments to the Labour Code' (hereinafter, LC RF (2001)) was adopted. It included a special section 54.1 (Article 348.1-348.12) regulating the employment of professional sportsmen and women. Following the same logic as the 'Law on Sport', it avoids to provide a definition of professional sportsman and defines sportsmen as workers whose labour function consists in preparation and participation in competitions on certain kind(s) of sport (Article 348(1)). Despite its undoubted role in improving the general legal framework regulating sport, however it still leaves some lacunas, especially with regard to such controversial issues as the transfer of sportsmen and women, and the termination of employment contracts which due to the substantial financial implications often leads to litigation at national and international level. Some of them are regulated by the norms of national sports federations that are intended to comply with the norms of the international federations. Sports federations usually have their own regulations, and disputes relating to sport are often resolved within the federations through internal dispute resolution bodies.[28]

41. In this relation some legal scholars raise practical questions regarding the limits of such an autonomy of sport federations within the framework of Russian legal system. In particular they ask if the norms of the federation are obligatory for the subjects involved in sport activity and to which extent they are allowed to derogate from the federal laws. On the one hand LC RF states[29] that norms of sport federations must be taken into account by the employers in adoption of local normative acts so theoretically they are mandatory for the employers and their employees. However sport federations are not always direct employers of sportsmen so their regulations are not in this case local normative acts *strictu sensu* according to Article 8 of the LC RF. In this case if they are not transposed as local normative acts these regulations may not be obligatory.

28. It is a dubious point whether e the limitation of the rights of sportsmen in relation to their recourse to the ordinary may be considered to some extent as a worsening of employment conditions under the Russian labour law.
29. Article 348.1(3) LC RF.

42. On the other hand, Article 5 LC RF does not include customs and sport federations acts among sources of labour law.[30] According to general principle laid down in the Article 8 of LC RF local normative acts cannot worsen workers' employment conditions. However it is not clear what happens when some norms of the federations concern questions beyond their competences like for instance putting forward additional conditions for the conclusion of the employment contract.[31] In these cases it should depend on the decision of the authorized body (court or sport justice bodies) to judge about the legitimate nature of such norms.[32] In the opinion of some scholars the role of the local normative acts is still underestimated by the Russian legislator.[33]

43. Moreover special laws on occasion of important competitions or other world-scale events may be adopted. On occasion of the Sochi 2014 Olympiad an ad hoc Federal Law on 1 December 2007 N. 310-FZ 'On organization and caring out XXII Olympic winter games and XI Paralympics winder games in Sochi City in 2014 and development of the Sochi city as mountain climate resort and amendments in other legal acts of the RF' was adopted. Another example is the Federal Law from 7 June 2013 N 108-FZ 'on organization of FIFA World Cup Russia 2018' (already mentioned 'Football law'). These laws were contested by Russian trade unions as unconstitutional because of extensive derogations in terms of labour and immigration law and they even advanced a claim to eliminate special Article 351.2 of LC RF regarding the peculiarities of employment conditions of persons hired in relation to World Cup 2018.[34]

44. Since the Constitution (Article 72(1)) refers to general questions of physical culture and sport to the joint competence of the Russian Federation and its subjects, many of the subjects of the RF adopted their own special laws on sport. Among them the Law of Moscow from 26 June 1996 N. 20 ('On Physical culture and sport in Moscow'), the Law of St. Petersburg from 22 April 2002 N. 177-OZ ('On Physical culture and sport in St. Petersburg'), the Law of Novosibirsk oblast' from 25 July 2003 N. 128-OZ ('On Physical culture and sport in Novosibirsk oblast'), the Law of Omsk oblast' from 11 July 1995 N. 27-OZ ('On Physical culture and sport in Omsk oblast') and so on.

---

30. The acts of sport federations because of their specific nature and restricted circle of addressees were mentioned only in the Ch. 54.1.
31. For instance the requirement to stipulate the insurance policy to be admitted to sport activity.
32. O. A. Shevchenko, *Legal doctrine of labour regulation in professional sport and its realisation in Russia*, Dissertation, Moscow, 2014 (in Russian). (О. Шевченко, *Правовая доктрина регулирования труда в сфере профессионального спорта и пути ее реализации в России*, диссертация, М., 2014).
33. E. V. Pogosyan, *Forms of resolution of sport-related disputes*, Monograph, Wolters Kluwer, 2011, 12 (in Russian). (Погосян Е. В., *Формы разрешения спортивных споров*. Монография, Волтерс Клувер, 2011).
34. Possibilities to introduce unlimited working time, overtime, work on holidays, night work to derogate from minimum norms regarding wages and additional guarantees contemplated by labour legislation in this regard (Arts 154, 113, 153, 152 of LC RF). The organizations involved in World Cup 2018 preparation are also exempt from many norms of immigration law includes the right to invite foreign workers extra national quota and without work permits. In the opinion of the experts this creates a dangerous precedent and undermines the concept of decent work. *See* more http://trudprava.ru/expert/analytics/migrationanalyt/666.

Part I. Organization of Sport

Chapter 1. Public Regulation

§1. Sport and Tort Law

45. High risk of injuries is the intrinsic characteristic of sport. In general terms liability in tort is regulated by the Civil Code of the RF (Chapter 59 CC RF). According to the Article 1064 CC RF liability for damages incurred to a person lies on the person responsible for incurrence of damage and is subject to a full compensation to the injured person. Law can oblige to compensate damage also to a person different from one who directly incurred the damage. The liable person may be required to pay compensation in the amount superior to the level of the damage incurred. A liable person can be released from this duty in case of the proof of the absence of his/her fault. Even in the absence of the fault the liable person may be required to compensate the damage. Legal or natural persons who ensured their responsibility (both in case of compulsory or voluntary insurance) when the insurance amount is insufficient to cover the damage, should compensate the difference (Article 1072 CC). The damage incurred as a consequence of the legitimate actions must be compensated according to the laws in force. The compensation demand may be rejected if the damage was incurred upon the request or consent of the person who suffered the damage. According to the Article 1084 CC RF damage for life and health of a person during the contract performance must be compensated according to the Chapter 59 CC RF unless the law or the contract provide for a higher compensation level.

46. The amount of compensation may be increased by law or contract according to the Article 1085 CC RF. According to the Article 1086 CC RF, the amount of the lost income is determined in base of the percentage to the average monthly salary before the disablement or handicap and considering the degree of handicap. The lost income includes all kinds of income from labour and civil law contracts subject to the income tax. The forfeit payments including compensation for the non-used holidays or indemnity in case of termination of employment relationship and the income from the entrepreneurial activity or royalties are included in the concept of the lost income in base of the data from the tax inspection. All the incomes are calculated in gross amount before the tax payments. The average amount is calculated by division of the salary for the last twelve months by twelve. If the injured did not work at the moment when the damage was incurred, the salary of the last place where he/she had worked before the dismissal or an average salary of a worker with his qualification in the determined territory may be considered. In no case the amount of compensation may be lower than the amount of the average subsistence level for Russian Federation.[35]

47. In case of injury or handicap of a minor below the age of 14 years and young sportsmen of 14–18 years who do not receive any income, the liable person must compensate expenses for the medical treatment and for the lost or reduced capacity for work. For the purpose of determination of the amount, the average subsistence level in the RF is considered. If the injured person had a work-related income before the injury, it is taken into account in determining compensation which again in no case can be lower than the average subsistence level in the RF.

48. According to the Article 1090 CC RF, an injured person who partially lost his capacity for work may require a liable person an increased compensation at any time if his ability to work has worsened with respect to the time when the compensation had been awarded. Vice versa, a person liable for injury can claim for diminishing the compensation amount if the ability to work of the injured has improved respect to the time of the compensation award.

49. The injured person can claim the increase of compensation if the material situation of the liable person has improved while the amount of compensation was diminished according to Part 3 Article 1083 CC RF according to which the court can diminish the amount of compensation in relation to the material situation of the liable person (e.g., in case of pension or disability when the material state has deteriorated respect to the time of the compensation award) excluding the cases of intentional harm infliction. The amount of compensation is subject to indexation (Article 318 CC RF). The payments are usually performed on a monthly basis. In the exceptional circumstances the court may rule the forfeit payment but no more than for the three-year period.

50. In case of the company reorganization of the liable person (if it is the case of the legal person), according to the Article 1093 CC RF the liability related to compensation should pass to his successor. In case of the liquidation of the legal person all the payments must be capitalized and paid to the injured party according to the law in force.[36]

51. The peculiarity of liability in sport consists in its specific subjective composition which includes sportsmen, coaches, medical personnel, organizers of sport events, sport clubs, etc.[37] All these subjects can act both as claimants and defendants. Moreover in sport many injuries are inflicted unwittingly in course of sport practice.

---

35. The minimum wage is periodically adjusted and from 1 Jul. 2017 it is RUB 7,800 per month (Federal Law from 19.12.2016 N. 460-FZ) whereas the minimum subsistence level is RUB 10,701 per month (government Decree from 20 Jun. 2017 N. 730). The amount varies considerably in the regions reaching in some of them twice this figure but there is no formal obligation to adjust the subsistence level with the minimum wage. Federal regulations in this regard have never been adopted (Arts 133 and 421 LC RF).
36. Alekseyev, *supra* n. 17, 2012, 876–880.
37. A.V. Erofeev, *Peculiarities of Tort Liability in Sport*, in Vestnik of Volgograd University, Urisprud, 3(20), 2013 (in Russian). (А. В. Ерофеев., *Об особенностях деликтной ответственности в области спорта* // Вестник Волгоградского Государственного Университета, Юриспруд. N. 3 (20), 2013.

52. As it has been mentioned, according to the Article 1085 CC RF if a sportsman had incurred a damage or handicap he must be compensated by the liable person his lost income and additional expenses related to his/her health conditions including medical treatment, costs of medicines, prosthetics, acquisition of special transportation, eventual training for another professional carrier if necessary, etc. The necessity in these treatments and impossibility to obtain them free of charge must be duly certified by the injured person. Disability pension or other compensatory payments assigned before and after injury do not affect the amount of the compensation due, as well as any sort of income received by the injured after the health damage.

53. Theoretically choosing a sport-related carrier and a particular kind of sport (which may be more dangerous and traumatic in respect to others) and signing a contract, professional sportsman implicitly admits the possibilities of future injuries. In determination of the degree of fault and material liability the degree of intent of culpable person must be considered in relation to specific kind of sport, including natural risks and violation of the rules of the game. Another important legal aspect is that if a sportsman acts in base of the written with the club (sport organization) employment agreement so the latter must be recognized liable for the compensation of harm (Article 1068 CC RF). In this case the club can regressively ask the tortfeasor the compensation. More problematic in this regard may be a situation when a sportsmen has a civil law contract with the sport organization. However in any case it is a sport organization which should be responsible for any harm or injury as in many cases it is difficult to identify a tortfeasor (for instance in case of launching a petard from the stadium from the tribunes). In this case the imperfection of Russian legal regulation creates difficulties for the victims to require a due compensation.

54. In case of sport-related injury the injured sportsman can claim moral damage according to Article 151 CC RF. In this case the court takes into consideration the degree of fault of the liable person as well as the degree of physical and moral pains of the injured person considering individual characteristics and factual and other circumstances related to injury without prejudice to the principles of reasonableness and fairness (Article 1101 CC RF).

55. Moreover according to the Article 34.6 of the 'Law on Sport',[38] All-Russian sport federations and accredited sport federations are authorized to carry out control over the observance of the federal standards of sport training by sport organizations and defend the rights of the injured sportsmen.

56. Generally it would be appropriate to improve the modality of sport-related disputes resolution and precise the extent of liability considering peculiarities of each kind of sport as well as to envisage the improvement of the system of obligatory insurance against possible risks especially in case of civil law contracts.

§2. Organizers of Sport Event

57. Pursuant to Federal Law 329-FZ of 4 December 2007 ('Law on Sport') the organizer of sports events is a legal person who approves the sports competition regulations, determines its conditions and scheduling, admission conditions, way of

38. Provision of the Ministry of Sport from 16 Aug. 2013, N. 636.

determining the best participant(s), organizational order of competition, competition funding and carries out other functions according to the Federal Law 'On Sport'.

58. The organizers of sport events have a set of responsibilities in relation to the events organization. Article 2 of the 'Law on Sport' regulates the main notions in the sphere of competitions.

59. Each sport organization adopts normative acts regulating competition activity. Normally there are special regulations for each kind of sport. The Decree of the Ministry of Sport from 1 July 2013 N 504 lays down common standards for the regulations on interregional and All-Russian sports events and competitions.[39] Normally they are prepared for each event. They should include general terms (reasons and aims of event), place and duration, requisites of organizers, requirements to the participants and conditions of access, event programme, conditions of results, awards, conditions of funding, safety measures, insurance issues, etc. They also specify rights and obligations and their division among the organizers.

60. Pursuant to the Article 20 of the 'Law on Sport', the organizers of sport events determine their conditions including compensation for travelling, food, equipment and referees fees. Moreover, they are responsible for all the organizational aspects and have a right to change the terms of the competitions or decide to terminate them. They also bear responsibility for the confirmation of the competitions results. In addition, they have exclusive rights regarding the name and symbolics as well as advertisement rights for the completions and their broadcasting in mass media. Third parties may acquire these rights only on the base of the agreement with the organizers.

61. All the organizers (if there are more than one) together with the owners and other users of the sport infrastructures (Article 20(1.9) have joint responsibility for safety provisions during sport events and injuries incurred to participants or third parties in course of competitions.

62. International sport competitions on the territory of the RF[40] can be carried out only upon the consent of the All-Russian sport federations on kinds of sport concerned, executive authorities of the subjects of the RF on which territory the events are carried out and the Ministry of Sport of the RF. The organization of all sport official competitions is possible only on condition of inclusion in the panel of organizers of All-Russian sport federations or representatives from the federal executive body in the field of physical culture and sport (Article 20(15) 'Law on Sport'). Normally the organizers should observe the following matters:

- establish organizing committee, professional staff and volunteers;
- adopt competition regulations;
- determine the place of the event;
- establish the referee college and carry out all necessary support for its functioning;
- verify the place where the event will be carried out;
- propose the scenario of opening/closing event;

39. Abrogates the previous provision of the Ministry of Sport from 8 May 2009 N 290 which laid down common standards for the regulations on interregional and All-Russian sports events and competitions.
40. With the exception of military and service applied kinds of sport.

- organize reception, travels, food and provide other support for competition participants;
- ensure medical support of the competitions and necessary health and safety measures;
- prepare the prizes and prize fund;
- carry out advertising campaigns.[41]

§3. Sport Medicine

63. According to the Olympic Charter (rule 2) the protection of the health of sportsmen and women is a priority of the IOC. For this reason the IOC has a special medical commission in charge of implementing anti-doping rules, controls and directives on the medical treatment of sportsmen and women. The main principles and guidelines on medical assistance in sport are laid down in the World Medical Association (WMA) Declaration on Principles of Health Care for Sports Medicine adopted in Lisbon in 1981 by the 34th World Medical Association General Assembly.[42] It states in particular:

> Considering the involvement of physicians in sports medicine, the WMA recommends the following ethical guidelines for physicians in order to help meet the needs of athletes, recognizing the special circumstances in which their medical care and health guidance is given.
>
> Consequently,

(1) The physician who cares for athletes has an ethical responsibility to recognize the special physical and mental demands placed upon them by their performance in sports activities.
(2) When the sports participant is a child or an adolescent, the physician must give first consideration to the participant's growth and stage of development:

   (a) The physician must ensure that the child's state of growth and development, as well as his or her general condition of health can absorb the rigors of the training and competition without jeopardizing the normal physical or mental development of the child or adolescent.
   (b) The physician must oppose any sports or athletic activity that is not appropriate to the child's stage of growth and development or general condition of health. The physician must act in the best interest of the health of the child or adolescent, without regard to any other interest or pressure from any other source.

41. Alekseyev, *supra* n. 17, 2012, 631.
42. Reaffirmed by the 185th WMA Council Session, Evian-les-Bains, France, May 2010.

(3) When the sports participant is a professional athlete and derives livelihood from that activity, the physician should pay due regard to the occupational medical aspects involved.

(4) The physician should be aware that the use of doping practices by a physician is a violation of the medical oath and the basic principles of the WMA's Declaration of Geneva, which states: 'My patient's health will always be my first consideration.' The WMA considers the problem of doping to be a threat to the health of athletes and young people in general, as well as being in conflict with the principles of medical ethics. The physician must thus oppose and refuse to administer or condone any such means or method which is not in accordance with medical ethics, and/or which might be harmful to the athlete using it, especially:

(a) Procedures which artificially modify blood constituents or biochemistry.
(b) The use of drugs or other substances whatever their nature and route of administration, including central nervous system stimulants or depressants and procedures which artificially modify reflexes.
(c) Pharmacological interventions that may induce alterations of will or general mental outlook.
(d) Procedures to mask pain or other protective symptoms if used to enable the athlete to take part in events when lesions or signs are present which make his participation inadvisable.
(e) Measures which artificially change features appropriate to age and sex.
(f) Training and taking part in events when to do so would not be compatible with preservation of the individual's fitness, health or safety.
(g) Measures aimed at an unnatural increase or maintenance of performance during competition. Doping to improve an athlete's performance is unethical.

(5) The physician should inform the athlete, those responsible for him or her, and other interested parties, of the consequences of the procedures the physician is opposing, guard against their use, enlist the support of other physicians and other organizations with the same aim, protect the athlete against any pressures which might induce him or her to use these methods and help with supervision against these procedures.

(6) The sports physician has the duty to give his or her objective opinion on the athlete's fitness or unfitness clearly and precisely, leaving no doubt as to his or her conclusions.

(7) In competitive sports or professional sports events, it is the physician's duty to decide whether the athlete is medically fit to remain on the field or return to the game. This decision cannot be delegated to other professionals or to other persons. In the physician's absence these individuals must adhere strictly to the instructions he or she has given them, with priority always being given to the best interests of the athlete's health and safety, and not the outcome of the competition.

(8) In order to carry out his or her ethical obligations the sports physician must see his or her authority fully recognized and upheld, particularly wherever it concerns the health, safety and legitimate interests of the athlete, none of which can be prejudiced to favour the interests of any third party whatsoever. These principles

and obligations should be supported by an agreement between the sports physician and the athletic organization involved, recognizing that the physician is obligated to uphold the ethical principles determined in national and international statements to which the medical profession has subscribed and by which it is bound.

(9) The sports physician should endeavour to keep the patient's personal physician fully informed of facts relevant to his or her treatment. If necessary the sports physician should collaborate to ensure that the athlete does not exert himself or herself in ways detrimental to his or her health and does not use potentially harmful techniques to improve performance.

(10) In sports medicine, as in all other branches of medicine, professional confidentiality must be observed. The right to privacy over medical attention the athlete has received must be protected, especially in the case of professional athletes.

(11) The sports doctor must not be party to any contract which obliges him or her to reserve particular forms of therapy solely and exclusively for any one athlete or group of athletes.

(12) It is desirable that sports physicians from foreign countries, when accompanying a team in another country, should enjoy the right to carry out their specific functions.

(13) The participation of a sports physician is desirable when sports regulation is being drawn up.[43]

64. In Russia, the 'Law on Sport' regulates a number of issues relating to the insurance of health and safety in sport. In particular Article 3(6) establishes the principle of health and safety of sportsmen and women, spectators and other participants in sport events, while under Article 6(10) of the same law, the Russian Federation is granted powers relating to physical culture and sport including medical care for Russian national teams. Article 10(2) establishes that physical culture organizations should ensure for sportsmen and women and their coaches all necessary health and safety provisions. Article 34 of the 'Law on Sport' is dedicated to federal standards of sports training, and also deals with certain matters in the medical field. In particular Article 34(1.6) states that organizations that provide training should ensure health and safety of participants, including investigation of incidents during training, and incidents occurring during sports competitions. Article 34(4) sets forth the duties and the responsibilities of persons taking part in sports training, stating that these persons have a right to medical support as well as an obligation to carry out necessary medical check-ups and follow medical instructions in a timely manner. Moreover they must inform responsible persons of any real or potential threats to their health and safety and that of other persons, and about any public order violations during sporting events. Article 34(5) regulates medical support of sportsmen.[44] Pursuant to this article a person who wishes to engage in sports training must present the documents confirming that he/she has successfully passed the necessary medical control as laid down by the federal laws.

Under Article 39(1) of the 'Law on Sport' medical support for individuals practising sport includes:

43. http://www.wma.net/en/30publications/10policies/h14/.

44. Articles 34(5) and 34(6) were introduced by Federal Law N 412-FZ, 6 Dec. 2011.

- systematic control of their state of health;
- evaluation of the physical efforts in relation to their state of health;
- prevention and medical treatment of diseases and injuries;
- rehabilitation by means of adequate techniques.

65. Under Article 39(2) of the 'Law on Sport', the organizers of sport events are required to ensure medical support and assistance for participants at sporting events.

An important provision of an exceptional nature is contained in Article 39(3) which states that during sporting events on the RF territory, professionals in possession of a medical or pharmaceutical qualification awarded abroad who are recognized as medical personnel by foreign states are entitled to provide medical support for sportsmen and women from these states on the RF territory defined by the event organizers without any requirement to follow the procedures allowing access to the practise of the medical profession laid down by the laws of the RF.

66. Decree No. 337, 20.08.2001, issued by the Ministry of Health of the RF 'On measures for further development and promotion of sports medicine and curative physical culture', sets forth a series of measures to ensure coordination and unification of the activity of medical organizations in relation to sport and physical culture to increase the effectiveness of preventive measures and improve the state of health by means of sport. To achieve these goals the following acts were adopted as annexes to the provision:

- Main directions of medical support of physical culture and sport, prevention of diseases and rehabilitation of sick and disabled persons by means of physical culture and sport (Annex 1).
- Provision on medical support of people practising physical culture and sport (Annex 2).
- Programme of in-depth medical check-ups of sportsmen and women of the national Russian teams and of their reserve players (Annex 3).
- Instruction on implementation of the programme of in-depth medical check-ups of sportsmen of national Russian teams and their reserve players (Annex 4).
- Programme of medical check-ups of persons practising mass sport and physical culture (Annex 5).
- Establishment of the expert council on curative physical culture and sports medicine of the Ministry of Health of RF (Annex 6).
- Composition of the expert council on curative physical culture and sports medicine of the Ministry of Health of RF (Annex 7).
- Provisions on work organization of the medical health centre of physical culture (Annex 8).
- Provision on the work of sports medicine department (Annex 9).
- Provision on functioning of physical culture department (Annex 10).
- Provision on functioning of organization and methods department (Annex 11).
- Provision on sports physicians (Annex 12).
- Provision on the work conditions and requirement of sport physicians (Annex 13).

- Provision on the work conditions and requirements of instructors of curative physical culture (Annex 14).
- Provision on the work of instructors of curative physical culture (Annex 15).
- Provision on the work conditions and requirements of nurses and masseurs (Annex 16).
- Norms regulating the workload of specialists in physical culture and sport (Annex 17).

67. Annex 3 to the Ministry of Health Decree No. 337 approved the programme of in-depth medical examinations for sportsmen and women, members of the Russian national teams and their reserve players which includes standard lists of medical check-ups obligatory for leading sportsmen and women, the level of their efficiency and necessary adjustments for training and rehabilitation of functions in order to achieve optimal results.

This programme is obligatory for all medical organizations carrying out check-ups on sportsmen and women regardless of their departmental affiliation and the legal status of the organization.

The programme includes:

- in-depth check-ups;
- complex examinations;
- examinations including medical and pedagogical tests;
- examinations during competition periods.

68. The aim of in-depth medical examinations is to obtain information on the state of health, physical development and functional abilities of sportsmen and women and national team members at all stages of training.

69. The tasks of the in-depth medical check-ups are:

- to analyse the health and functional state of the body and the physical development of sportsmen and women;
- to determine risk factors in relation to their health, any decline of physical activity and abilities in relation to a certain kind of sport, individual characteristics and training regimes;
- to diagnose chronic diseases relevant for the functioning of the body and sports efficiency;
- to carry out diagnostics and assess physical efficiency considering the various stages of training;
- to determine the level of functional preparation considering the state of health of individual training plans;
- to determine access to training and competitions by sportsmen and women on the basis of their state of health;
- to adopt recommendations to increase adaptation possibilities, prevention, curative and other measures.

70. The programme is adopted for five kinds of sport:

(1) cyclical;
(2) speed-strength based;
(3) combat sports;
(4) sports games;
(5) coordination sports.

71. The programme of examination includes:

(1) medical examination by:

- a sports physician;
- specialists including therapists, trauma surgeons, neurologists, dentists, ear nose and throat specialists, oculists, gynaecologists, endocrinologists, neuropsychiatrists and urologists.

(2) laboratory examinations:

- complete blood count;
- urine tests;
- clinical and biochemical analysis of blood for:

  (a) determination of regulators of energetic metabolism: cortisol, testosterone, insulin;
  (b) determination of the thyroid status: T3 general, T4 general TTG (thyrotropin);
  (c) determination of the level of enzymes (alanine transaminas, creatine phosphokinase, (d) alkaline phosphatase;
  (e) determination of biochemical indicators (glucose, holestirin, triglycerides,
  (f) phosphorus, sexual health indicators (for young sportsmen and women).

(3) testing of general work efficiency:

- bicycle exercise test or treadmill running at maximum speed in cyclical sports and games;
- bicycle exercise test PWC-170 for combat sports, speed-strength based and coordination sports.

The heart rate is measured before and after the test along with arterial blood pressure.

72. Annex 4 to the Decree No. 337 laid down the requirement for in-depth medical examinations of sportsmen and women of national teams and reserve players defining the modality of the implementation of the programme of in-depth examinations.

Such examinations include:

- preliminary tests to determine access to high-level professional sport;
- periodical tests to be administered once a year.

73. In-depth medical check-ups including preliminary and periodical tests must be carried out at regular intervals. Landmark medical check-ups at different stages of training, including medical and pedagogical tests, can be administered less frequently considering the activities to be performed. Preliminary in-depth examinations are carried out before the selection of the team or reserve players, while periodical in-depth tests are to be administered once a year. Landmark examinations may be administered 2–4 times a year and should be adapted to particular tasks or kinds of sport.

74. Ongoing medical examinations should be carried out throughout the year to assess the state of health and adaption to the training workload.[45]

75. The Decree of the Ministry of Health and Social Development of Russia, No. 613, 9 August 2010, required the provision of medical assistance during competitions.[46] Pursuant to this measure sports physicians should carry out their activity in a medical unit at the event of the team or the club. They should ensure medical assistance for sportsmen and women during sporting events, manage access sportsmen and women to training and competitions and monitor their state of heath. Another important task is the prevention of doping and supervision of the dietary regime. Sports physicians have an obligation of confidentiality.[47] Many of the provisions duplicate those of Decree No. 337 which since it has not been officially repealed continues to be applied at least with regard to those parts that do not contradict the provisions of Decree No. 613 and other legal norms in force.

76. Special acts can be adopted in relation to major international competitions. For example on the occasion of the Sochi 2014 Olympic Games the Decree of the Ministry of Health No. 835н, 11.11.2013, 'On the modality of the medical assistance to the sportsmen, members of Olympic family, spectators, staff, mass media representatives and participants of the opening and closing ceremony during the Sochi 2014 Olympics' was adopted.

77. Until 2009, medical insurance for top-level professional sportsmen and women was provided by the Ministry of Sport. Pursuant to government Decree No. 812, 17 October 2009, the responsibility for medical insurance was transferred to the system of the executive bodies of RF – the Ministry of Health and Social Development of Russia[48] and its federal subordinated agency (the Federal Medical and Biological Agency, FMBA).[49] On the basis of this provision this agency regulates medical services for national teams of the RF and reserve players and their preliminary and periodical medical controls. It is also responsible for the coordination of the activity of sports medicine institutions in the RF. Not all the sports federations supported this change. Some of them argued that sports medicine should have remained under the Ministry of Sport and that in this way 'medicine did not come to sport while sport was deprived

45. Y. V. Stukalova, *Commentary* to the Ch. 54.1 of the Russian Labour Code 'Peculiarities of the regulation of labour of sportsmen and coaches', Garant system, 2009. (Ю. В. Стукалова, *Комментарий* к главе 54.1 Трудового кодекса Российской Федерации "Особенности регулирования труда спортсменов и тренеров" (постатейный), Система Гарант, 2009.
46. Decree No. 613 9 Aug. 2010 'On the modality of medical assistance during sports events'.
47. Alekseyev, 2012, *supra* n. 17, 830–847.
48. https://www.rosminzdrav.ru/.
49. http://fmbaros.ru/special/activities/sport_medicine/.

of medicine'.[50] Many leading medical institutions that are not part of the FMBA were excluded from working with national teams which in view of the general shortage of staff in the field of sports medicine[51] might be to the detriment of the sportsmen. Medical treatment and rehabilitation of the leading sportsmen and women is often provided thanks to funding from regional ministries of sport, All-Russian sport federations or the personal funds of sportsmen. The Ministry of Sport (Minsport) collaborates closely with the FMBA with the aim of improving the quality of medical support for sportsmen and women. A number of normative acts have been adopted in course of this collaboration such as the above-mentioned Decree No. 613 by the Ministry of Health and Social Development of Russia, Decree No. 3 of 2013 'On medical and medico-biological support of national sport teams of the RF' and Decree No. 916н 'On approval of the unified qualification directory of the professional positions in the sphere of physical culture and sport'.

78. The 'Law on Sport' does not define the legal status of sport physicians. Medical personnel are assigned to work with the teams but members of medical profession are not included in the national teams and consequently they are not covered by the provisions concerning presidential scholarships and bonuses in relation to the competition results of Olympics and Paralympics and World and Europe championships.[52]

79. In relation to the status of medical personnel in the field of sports medicine and their qualifications, the following normative acts are relevant:

- the Decree of the Ministry of Health, No. 434, 16 September 2003 'On the approval of qualifications of the physician in curative physical culture and sport medicine';
- the Decree of the Ministry of Health No. 415н, 7 July 2009, establishing qualification requirements for medical professionals with a higher degree. Pursuant to this provision, basic medical education should last for six years, with specialization in Paediatrics or in Medicine with an obligatory specialization in sports medicine. Sports physicians are required to update their qualifications every five years;
- the Decree of the Ministry of Health and Social Development of Russia, No 541, 23 July 2010 'On the approval of the unified qualification directory of the professional positions of chief executives, specialists and employees (section dedicated to the qualifications of employees in the medical profession)' approves the professional characteristics of sports physicians. They have a duty to carry out in-depth medical clinical examinations of sportsmen and women, including sportsmen and women with a disability. Moreover sports physicians are required to know the Russian Constitution and other laws in the field of heath, the principles of organization of sports medicine, health and safety norms, labour law, peculiarities of work under pressure, age peculiarities, contraindications for practising sports

50. *See* D. Rogachev, *Legal regulation of medical support of sport competitions*, materials of the *VIII* annual international conference on actual problems of improving of legal regulation in the sphere of physical culture and sport, 30 May, 2014, Moscow.
51. According to the report by the Minister of Health and Social Development of the RF, T. Golikova dated 20 Jul. 2010 (http://minsport-mari.ru/archives/1386=) in 2008 for every sports physician there were 7065 persons practising sport. In addition for one institution of physical culture and sport medicine there were more than 51,000 persons practising sport.
52. Alekseyev, 2012, *supra* n. 17, 834.

and so on. The same decree establishes the requirements for masseurs. They should have professional qualifications (not necessarily a higher degree) with specializations such as medicine, obstetrics and nursing and a diploma in massage for medicinal purposes. They should also have a knowledge of the foundations of the Russian legal system, the principles of applying massage to curative physical culture and various kinds of massage;

- the Decree of the Ministry of Health and Social Development of Russia, N. 916н, 15 August 2011 'On approval of the unified qualification directory of the professional positions of chief executives, specialists and employees' (section dedicated to the qualifications of employees in the sphere of sport) establishes the qualifications for sports physicians of the national sport teams of the RF (in relation to different kinds of sport) and masseurs of the national teams.

80. In addition, sports medicine is subject to licensing, and the Order of the Ministry of Sport and Social Development, No. 1664, 27 December 2011 established a nomenclature of health services and attributed to each kind of service a particular code.[53]

81. Another important legal source where a reference to sports medicine is to be found is the Labour Code of the Russian Federation (LC RF). Article 348.3 LC RF regulates medical check-ups for sportsmen and women. Before concluding an employment contract, sportsmen are required to undergo an obligatory medical examination. During their employment they are subject to periodical medical check-ups in order to ascertain and prevent occupational diseases.

82. Employers are under an obligation to organize at their own expense obligatory preliminary and annual periodical medical examinations, extra medical check-ups at the request of players and medical advice. Players continue to receive their salary during absences for medical check-ups. Sportsmen are obliged to attend these check-ups and follow medical advice. Analogous provisions are contained in the regulations on the Status and Transfer of Players (Article 7(12) for the players and Article 7(14) for the clubs).

83. A refusal by sportsmen and women to undergo these check-ups is deemed to be a breach of discipline with corresponding sanctions, while repeated avoidance without justified reason may result in legitimate dismissal. According to Article 76 LC RF, the employer is required to exempt from work an employee who has not passed an obligatory check-up. In cases in which failure to pass a medical check-up can be imputed to a fault on the part of the player, the player is not paid for the entire period up to the check-up. If players fail to pass a check-up for reasons not depending on their own actions, they are paid two-thirds of normal salary as in the case of obligatory exemption from work.

84. Medical support for sport events may be regulated also at the level of the subjects of the RF by means of special laws.[54] The relative measures are supposed to be funded from the budgets of the bodies of the RF concerned or by the organizers of the sports event.

53. Rogachev, *supra* n. 50, 2014.
54. For instance Act No. 27, 15 Jun. 2009 'On physical culture and sport in Moscow'.

85. Also sports federations and leagues can adopt special norms in relation to sports medicine. One of the best examples in this regard is the medical regulation of the Kontinental Hockey League (KHL).[55] This regulation contains detailed norms in relation to medical support for the clubs, an online medical portal, licensing requirements for medical activity, qualification requirements for the physicians, requirements for medical equipment,[56] regulations concerning doping test procedures, medical examinations and a decision-making procedure in the case of health problems of players. This is one of the most advanced regulations but it still represents an exception rather than the norm and in many federations such regulations are far less detailed or completely absent.

86. The Strategy for the development of physical culture and sport in the RF till 2020 adopted by the Russian government established a set of measures in order to improve the situation in this field. These measures are intended to promote the following aims:

- to modernize the system of scientific, methodological, medical, biological, psychological and pedagogical support of national teams and sports reserves;
- to promote the role of health centres in the diagnosis of the state of health of sportsmen and women;
- to optimize the system of medical and biological support of sportsmen in national teams and reserve players;
- to set up temporary scientific centres for the scientific and methodological support of the national teams;
- to adopt a set of measures to improve anti-doping measures in top-level professional sport and among reserve players;
- to design and implement a system of training and certification of coaches and physicians of the Olympics and Paralympics national teams and teams of the bodies of the RF to combat doping;
- to strengthen the accountability of sportsmen, coaches and medical staff in relation to doping;
- to design and implement medical support in sports competitions.

87. Governmental Decree No. 294, 15.04.2014, lays down the goal of providing 100% of the national teams with physicians and masseurs in the coming years.

§4. Hooliganism and Problems of Security of Sport Events

88. Sport hooliganism is undoubtedly a sore point of Russian professional sport, in particular of football. Hooligans are people who violate public order because of their football tastes and preferences. The other category are fans who can be defined

55. Approved by the KHL directory board, protocol No. 38, 19 Aug. 2014.
56. Pursuant to Art. 6, it must contain an automatic defibrillator. Moreover all the medicines must be in compliance with the requirements of the national legislation and have instructions in Russian, and for foreign clubs in their national language. The detailed list of medicines is specified in annex 2 to the Regulation.

as persons whose beliefs or behaviour involves uncritical zeal or an obsessive enthusiasm for a pastime or hobby. In general terms the phenomenon of fanaticism can be defined as a specific subculture whose representatives share certain common traditions and values. While the word 'hooligan' has a negative semantic connotation, fans can be characterized both positively and negatively. Hooliganism can be defined as an extreme (illegal) manifestation of fanaticism. In practice hooligans and fans are often used in Russian football related literature as synonyms. For simplicity reasons we will do the same in this chapter. Both fans and hooligans as well as other ultras may use banners, pyrotechnics, sing the hymns during the matches.[57] They may justify their aggressive behaviour by the 'noble' intentions to defend the 'honour' of their clubs against the other clubs. However often hooliganism and fanaticism is linked to racism, fascism and other forms of xenophobia.

89. Hooliganism originates from Great Britain. In Russia the first wave was registered in the 1970s in relation to the conflict during the Spartak's match when the fans were badly treated by local police (the then *militzia*). The repressions however only provoked its further expansion which became even stronger after the collapse of the Soviet regime. Now these movements exist in almost all the cities and their number has grown up with respect to the past.

90. Unfortunately there are number of unpleasant incidents related to football hooliganism. On 9 June 2002 after the match between Russia and Japan in Moscow mass riots took place at Manezhnaya square with 50 people injured, 1 dead, 106 damaged cars. In March 2005 in Mahachkala after the match between Anzhi (Mahachkala) and Dinamo (Mahachkala) there was a riot between the fans of both teams.[58] Another one relates to the fight between police and fans in 2008 during the match between Zenit and Dinamo when an extremely offensive banner against a dead famous ex Soviet player Lev Yashin was exposed.[59] Among the recent most resounding cases is one that happened in November 2013 during the match between Dinamo and Zenit at Khimki stadium when from the guest sector a petard was thrown to Dinamo gate. The goalkeeper, Anton Shunin, was severally injured with a cornea burnt. Among the sanctions Zenit was awarded a defeat on technical grounds. In 2015 during the match on 27 March between Montenegro and Russia a flare was thrown by a Montenegro fan hitting Russian goalkeeper Igor Akinfeev who had to be transported off the field on a stretcher, and fortunately suffered small burns of his neck, as well as a mild concussion. UEFA sanctioned Chernogoria with two matches behind the closed doors and Zenit with a fine of EUR 25,000 while the fan who hit Akinfeev received 3.5 months of imprisonment.

91. These are just few examples and the list of course could be much longer. All these accidents have exacerbated the necessity to create a sound legal framework for the prevention of hooligans behaviour in organization of sport events in line with the international standards.

---

57. Not only official hymns of the clubs but also the songs created by the fans, a kind of folklore.
58. V. V. Saraev, *Criminal law protection of contemporary professional sport in Russia*, Dissertation, Omsk, 2009 (in Russian). (В. В. Сараев, *Уголовно-правовая охрана современного профессионального спорта в России*, Диссертация, Омск, 2009).
59. http://newsland.com/news/detail/id/31772point.

92. Russia ratified European Convention 'On prevention of violence and misbehaviour during sport events and football matches'.[60] By this Convention, the contracting parties commit themselves to take all necessary measures for the implementation of this Convention and to coordinate the policy and the activities of their ministries and other state agencies against spectator violence and misbehaviour, by forming coordinating bodies where possible. The Convention stipulates a series of measures to be ensured by contracting parties including legal, punitive, administrative, organizational, technical and even social and educational ones. In order to implement these measures an appropriate coordination between different stakeholders including state bodies, courts, prosecutors and sports clubs and their owners is necessary.

93. Special sanctions may be established also at the level of sport federations. So Article 100 of the Disciplinary Regulations of FUR (2010) states that in case of provoking of spectators by the players or club officials which create a treat of disorders on the stadium, one match disqualification or fine can be applied (as defined in the clause 20 of the Annex 1 to the regulations). In case where players' or club officials' provocative actions brought to the disorders, the disqualification of five matches plus fine can be sanctioned (clause 21 of the Annex 1).

94. If the receiving party did not take necessary measures to ensure public order and safety at the stadium (Article 101) and such an omission brought to the violations of public order and created threats to the safety, the fine is applied pursuant to the clause 22 of the Annex 1. In case of more serious consequences, such sanctions as the prohibition to the spectators to accede to the stadium sectors for one to five matches or a match under the closed door or at the neutral stadium in a different city (from one to five matches) may be ordered.

95. Finally a special Law 'On fans' behaviour' (entered into force 20 January 2014) was adopted.[61] Its provisions were further specified in the governmental regulation from 16 December 2013 N 1156 'On the approval of the rules of spectators behaviour during official sport competitions'. These acts establish the responsibility not only for the fans but also for the competition organizers, owners of the stadiums and other legal and physical persons involved.

96. Pursuant to this law, it is prohibited to appear drunk in official sites of sport competitions, throw objects, insult other people, hide the face under the mask and threat public order in any other way. Moreover it is prohibited to bring any arms, pyrotechnics or other tools which may cause inflammation or smoke. Also some musical instruments (like vuvuzela) are prohibited (fifes and bugles are admitted). Flags, banners and other supporting measures cannot contain political or extremist signs, Nazi symbols or other offensive signs. Foreign expressions must be translated into Russian and duly notarized and checked at the entrance. Fans must also present an identity document when required.

97. The law provides sanctions including administrative fines, obligatory works, prohibition to assist football matches in future. The violation of the rules of behaviour on the stadiums is punished by the fine ranging within RUB 3 up to RUB 10,000 or

60. European Convention on Spectator Violence and Misbehaviour at Sports Events and in particular at Football Matches ETS N 120 (Strasbourg, 19 Aug. 1985).
61. Federal Law of 23 Jul. 2013, N. 192-FZ, 'On the amendments to the single legislative acts of the RF in relation to the guarantee of public order and safety during official sport competitions'.

obligatory works up to 160 hours with prohibition to assist the matches for a period from six months to three years. In case of recidivism the fine may amount to RUB 15,000 or arrest up to fifteen days. As a last resort, the violator may be prohibited to assist the matches up to seven years. This measure must be decided in the court. The most malicious offenders will be included in the black lists and managed by the federal executive services of the Ministry of Internal Affairs.

The fines may be applied not only to fans but also to the event organizers and owners of football arenas. For the missed security arrangements they may be fined up to RUB 100,000 for physical persons and up to RUB 300,000 for the legal persons with possible arrest of the activity for a period up to ninety days. In case such actions brought to the harm of human health responsible administrative persons will be fined up to RUB 200,000 and legal persons up to RUB 500,000.

98. However the experts draw attention to the inconsistencies of this legal act. In particular they claim the lack of detailed description of infringement (as it seems there is no difference between throwing garbage in tribunes or more serious misbehaviour like attacking somebody) leaving this to the discretion of police. So since the kinds of infringements may vary significantly it seems inappropriate to establish so generic sanctions. In their opinion the problem is inadequately reflected in the Administrative Code. Even if governmental regulation from 16 December 2013 N 1156 described more concretely the kinds of infringements of the rules the problem has been still insufficiently regulated from the administrative point of view.[62]

99. Since these measures were apparently insufficient, especially in view of the World Cup 2018. Additional measures against hooliganism were introduced by Federal Law N. 78-FZ of 7 April 2017 introducing amendments to the Code of Administrative Offences and to the Law 'On Sport'. In particular clauses 3.6 and 3.7 were added to Article 4.1. of the Code of Administrative Offences as well as Article 20.25 and Article 20.31 while clause 14.1 was added to Article 20 of the Law on Sport. These measures mainly concern foreign citizens or stateless persons, and some of them may be limited only to the period of the official international sports competitions.

100. Article 3.7. envisages an administrative arrest of up to fifteen days with deportation from Russia in the case of violations of Article 20.31, clauses 4 and 5 Code of Administrative Offences if such violations took place during official international competitions.

101. Article 25.10, clause 3 of the Federal Law 114-FZ of 15 August 1996 states that a foreign nationals or stateless person may be banned from entering the territory of the Russian Federation if they breach the conditions laid down in Article 26 and 27 of the above-mentioned law.

62. The authors indicate that actually only Arts 20.31 and 20.32 of the Administrative Code of the RF regulate misbehaviour and problems of safety during sport competitions, I. V. Ponkin, A. A. Soloviev & A. I. Ponkina, *Legal protection against illegal behaviour of the sport fans*, Moscow, 2014, 46–50 (in Russian). (И. В. Понкин, А. А. Соловьев, А. И. Понкина, *Правовое обеспечение противодействия противоправному поведению спортивных болельщиков*, Москва, 2014, 46.50,)

102. Pursuant to Article 20.31, flagrant[63] violations on the part of spectators during official sports competitions, when not subject to criminal sanctions, are punished with an administrative fine between RUB 10,000 to 20,000 or to an administrative arrest up to fifteen days with a ban on attending sports competitions for a period up to seven years. In case in which these violations are committed by a foreign nationals or a stateless person the fine is from RUB 10,000 to 15,000 with deportation from the territory of the Russian Federation.

103. Article 4.1., clause 3.6, of the Code states that in case of administrative sanctions for the breach of Article 20.31 clauses 4 or 5 of the Code, the court may consider the length of the foreign national's or stateless person's stay in the Russian Federation, his/her family status, Russian tax payments, income, availability of accommodation, profession, compliance with the law, application for Russian citizenship and other circumstances. On the basis of the evaluation of these facts if the court considers deportation to be too severe and disproportionate a sanction, an administrative fine of RUB 40,000 to 50,000 or a ban on attending sport competitions from one to seven years may be applied.

104. Finally clause 14.1 of the Law 'On Sport' states that foreign nationals may be banned from entering Russia if there is information that in the past these people committed public order violations at international competitions in the territory of the Russian Federation or abroad or if they intend to do so during their stay in the territory of the Russian Federation.

105. Pursuant to the UEFA Clubs Licensing Statute and Financial Fair Play Regulations (Article 35), from the season 2012/2013, among other requisites for club licensing there is a presence of a supporter liaison officer. 'The licence applicant must have appointed a liaison officer to act as the key contact point for supporters. The supporter liaison officer must regularly attend meetings with the club's management and must collaborate with the security officer on safety and security-related matters.'[64] Following this requirement many Russian clubs introduced such a new professional qualification whose main duties include:[65]

- formation and promotion of fan culture;
- reorganization of structure of fan clubs;
- participation in the development of PR concept and advertisement campaigns aimed at promotion of fan loyalty;
- seminars and training for leaders of fan movement;
- preparation of budget for fan movement organization.

---

63. For the purpose of this law under the flagrant violations the following actions may be considered:
- actions threating public order, one's own or third persons' health and safety in place of sport competition or in the vicinity;
- violations of the rules on spectator' behaviour during official sports competitions resulting in suspension or arrest.

64. Art. 35 of the Statute of UEFA on Clubs Licensing Statute and Financial Fair Play Regulation (2010). *See also* in this regard UEFA Supporter Liaison Officer Handbook (2011)https://www.uefa.com/MultimediaFiles/Download/Tech/uefaorg/General/01/84/35/28/1843528_DOWNLOAD.pdf.

65. K. Gusov, O. Scevchenko, *Sports law*, Moscow, 2009, 62.

106. Sometimes they act simultaneously as press attaché to create a special brand for a club and image for an individual sportsman.[66]

107. Arguably, such negative phenomenon as sport violence and hooliganism can be prevented through the appropriate legal framework and proper implementation of the laws.

§5. Crowd Behaviour and Club Liability

108. Pursuant to the Article 20(1) of the 'Law on Sport' the organizers of sport events are liable for their carrying out the events (*see* §2 *supra*). The competitions must be organized according to the regulation on each competition which establishes specific rules. Russian legislation contemplates the sanctions in case of violations during sport events. The organizer has a certain discretion in allocating the responsibilities for the event organization and if necessary may engage also third persons in base of the competition regulation. He also may establish additional rules for the spectators behaviour which should not be in contrast with the federal laws. Normally in the absence of the special provisions in this regard the organizers have a joint responsibility in case of damage to the event participants or to the third persons. In addition to the sanctions specified in the paragraphs 97, 98 *supra*, according to the Article 238 of the Penal Code of the RF in case of non-insurance of safety during the sport events they can be punished with the fine up to RUB 300,000 or in the amount of the salary of the culpable person for two-year period or obligatory works from 120 up to 180 hours or imprisonment up to two years. The offenders may also be subject to administrative sanctions pursuant to the Administrative Code.

109. Federal Law from 23 July 2013 N 192 introduced some changes in the Law on Sport in relation to the responsibility of the organizers of sport events. It introduces a definition of spectator (Article 2(3.3) of the 'Law on Sport'), and a new professional figure – sport Stewart (Article 2(3.4) of the Law on Sport). Sport Stewart is defined as a natural person who has a special training in the field of physical culture and sport and who is engaged on the commercial basis by the sport event organizers or owners of the sport event facility in order to ensure public order and safety during the sport event. Article 20(2) of the 'Law on Sport' establishes professional requirements to the Stewarts and regulates their rights and duties. The following persons cannot be sport Stewards:

- persons without Russian citizenship;
- Russian citizens recognized by court decision unable to act or with limited ability to act;
- Russian citizens below the age of 18;
- persons with pending conviction or people to whom administrative sanctions according to the Article 20.31 of the Administrative Code were applied (for the period of the sanction duration);
- persons suffering mental disorders, alcoholism or drug dependency.

66. The activity of press attaché in Russia is regulated in the circular of Ministry of Labour from 28 Jul. 2003 N 59.

110. The Stewarts have a right to control the movements of the spectators before the beginning and after the end of the competitions, control entrance tickets, inform spectators about additional services they may require, prevent the entrance of persons to whom administrative prohibition of the court to assist at the sport event was adopted, inform the organizers of the sport events on any violation of the safety rules or incidents and where necessary, manage any emergency situations including evacuation of people.

111. Moreover the organizers of the sport events must ensure necessary infrastructure for the event including the systems of video surveillance and technical safety infrastructure, guarantee free access of the cars to the event including those of police and other services responsible for safety and ensure the possibilities of evacuation of people in case of emergency.

112. Regarding the sanctions for the infringement of public order *see* §4 *supra.*

Chapter 2. Dispute Resolution

113. Article 45(2) of the Russian Constitution grants all citizens the right to defend their personal rights and freedoms with recourse to all possible means not prohibited by law, whereas Article 46(1) of the Constitution safeguards the right to judicial protection as an inalienable personal right, and this applies also to relations in sport. Also the Labour Code of the RF grants all citizens the right to defend their employment rights and freedoms and lays down the right to judicial protection (Article 2 LC RF).

All those involved in sports or third parties have the right to apply to the bodies of general competence (regular courts) pursuant to the federal Constitutional Law of 31 December 1996 N. 1-FZ On the Judicial System of the Russian Federation. In the case of individual employment disputes at local level, if the employee wishes, he/she can refer the matter to special local commissions on labour disputes (Article 381–390 LC RF). Alternatively, they can refer the matter to special courts (arbitration courts) or use alternative procedures (such as mediation, independent expertise and others). Often sports-related disputes are regulated by the internal jurisdictional bodies of the federations (which may adopt their own mandatory provisions) but such an approach is not always suitable for sportsmen and women because of the question of impartiality of judgment and also because such bodies do not exist in all the sport federations. Finally, as a last resort, on condition that all the other means of judicial review have been exhausted at national level, it is possible to apply to the European Court of Human Rights in Strasbourg on the basis of the Convention for the Protection of Human Rights and Fundamental Freedoms ETS N. 005[67] or to the UN Human Rights Committee on the basis of the International Covenant on Political and Civil Rights (New York, 1966)[68] and optional protocols to this Covenant.[69]

Until recently there was no one single classification of sports-related disputes in the Russian legal literature[70] and no special provision on sports-related dispute resolution procedures existed in Labour Code or in the Law on Sport. This resulted in significant practical problems concerning the definition of the proper jurisdiction of a particular dispute. The recent reform of the arbitration system in Russia was intended to remedy these deficiencies and new legal acts in relation to sports disputes were adopted and proper amendments were introduced also into the Law on Sport as illustrated below.

Considering the specific nature of sport and sports-related disputes which require special competence of judges and rapid decision-making, various dispute resolution

67. Russia ratified this Convention by the Federal Law from 30 March N. 54-FZ 'On ratification of the Convention of Protection of Human Rights and Fundamental Freedoms and its protocols'. The Russian skiers Lasutina and Danilova appealed to the Court of Justice of the European Union against the decision to disqualify them for the use of doping and deprivation of the medals for the Olympics in 2002. However in 2007 they withdrew their appeal and no hearing was held. http://allsportinfo.ru/index.php?id=19741&b=15&l=40.
68. Entering into force for USSR on 23 Mar. 1976.
69. Entering in force for the Russian Federation on 1 Jan. 1992.
70. S. V. Alekseyev, *supra* n. 17, 2012, 971; *V.* Pogosyan, *supra* n. 33, 61–64.

procedures, including out-of-court settlements, have been developed in Russia. Such procedures include arbitration, mediation, conciliation (with an intermediary), preliminary expert evaluation by a neutral third party, independent expert opinion, a hybrid form of arbitration and mediation and recourse to the ombudsman.[71,72]

§1. Arbitration

114. Arbitration is one of a number of kinds of alternative dispute resolution procedures to deal with disputes by means other than litigation. Unlike litigation, arbitration takes place out of court and the parties commit themselves to complying with the arbitration award of an impartial arbitrator. The arbitrator's decision is deemed to be final, and cannot normally be re-examined by the regular courts.

The advantages of arbitration are widely recognized. The procedure is reasonably quick, which is important considering the relatively short careers of professional sportsmen and women. The parties can count on one or more arbitrators with specific competence in the field of sport (normally lacking in the ordinary courts) and they are free to choose them themselves. Arbitration decisions are considered to be final and not subject to appeal at a higher level. In addition, the procedure is less costly than proceedings in the regular courts, and details of the case are confidential.

The main principles of arbitration are as follows:

1 *independence and impartiality of the arbitrator*: arbitrators cannot represent the interests of one of the parties involved or be directly or indirectly interested in the decision on the case. They are required to inform the arbitration court immediately if they become aware of one of the above-mentioned problems;

2. *equality of the parties*: each party must have equal opportunities to present and defend their interests;

3. *competitiveness of the parties*: each party is expected to demonstrate the consequences that it cites in order to justify its claims;

4. *promotion by the arbitration court of an amicable agreement*: without violation of the rights and interests of the parties protected by law;

5. *confidentiality of the arbitration procedure*: arbitrators and their staff are not permitted to divulge the facts they become aware of during the arbitration procedure without the prior agreement of the interested parties. The arbitrator cannot be interrogated about these facts.

The right to file a complaint with the Court of Arbitration for Sport (CAS) is granted to all persons, either legal or natural, engaged primarily in sport, with or without the status of an individual entrepreneur.

71. Still current practice in the RF.
72. E. V. Pogosyan, *supra* n. 33, 40.

I. Arbitration Courts

115. The first two specialized arbitration courts for sport were set up in Moscow in 2003:

1 the CAS at the Russian Sports Chamber;[73]

2 the CAS at the Russian Chamber of Commerce and Industry.

In 2015 an important reform of the arbitration system was approved with greater attention being paid to sports arbitration. In this regard Federal Law No 382-FZ dated 29 December 2015, On Arbitration in the Russian Federation, was adopted, substituting the previous Federal Law N. 102 of 24 July 2002, On Courts of Arbitration in the Russian Federation, the norms of which have no longer been applicable since 1 September 2016 (except for cases initiated and not terminated at the time of entry in force).

This Law established a different procedure for setting up arbitration courts, subjecting them to government authorization.

First, it laid down a distinction between ad hoc arbitration courts (arbitration panels established on a temporary basis for the purpose of resolving a single dispute) and permanent arbitration bodies, laying down a number of obligatory criteria for permanent bodies. A permanent arbitration court or panel can be created only under the auspices of a non-commercial organization. Under Article 44(8) of Law N. 382-FZ, 2015, to qualify as a permanent arbitration body, a non-commercial organization is required to satisfy the following criteria:

- the regulations of the organization must conform to Federal Law N. 382-FZ, 2015;
- the list of recommended arbitrators must conform to Federal Law N. 382-FZ, 2015;
- the information in the application submitted by the non-commercial organization must be authentic;
- the organization is required to have a good reputation, including the reputation of its members, and the nature and scope of its activity as well as its financial resources, should enable it to carry out arbitration functions and to contribute to the development of the arbitration system in the RF.

The right to operate as a permanent arbitration body is granted by the RF government, on the recommendation of the national Council for the Improvement of Arbitration Procedures. A non-commercial organization has the right to appeal to the courts against the rejection of its application.

A foreign non-commercial organization can be granted the right to act as a permanent arbitration body on the RF territory provided it is widely recognized with an international reputation. In this case the requirements of Article 44 (8) are not subject to verification.

---

73. The Court of Arbitration for Sport at the Russian Sports Chamber was set up as an autonomous non-commercial body on 10 Jun. 2003 to deal with disputes about property rights including the status and transfer of players, disputes with agents, disputes regarding the decisions of sports organizations and disputes relating to doping.

On 27 January 2017 an International Commercial Arbitration Court (ICAS) at the Chamber of Commerce and Industry of the RF replaced the CAS at the Russian Chamber of Commerce and Industry.[74] The ICAS is regulated by the RF Federal Law N. 5338–1 of 7 July 1993, On International Commercial Arbitration (based on the UNCITRAL Model Law of 1985, as amended) and by Law N. 382-FZ, 2015 which recognized the court as a permanent arbitration body without the need to obtain governmental authorization (Article 44(1)).[75]

This Court has competence to deal with international sports disputes. According to the United Nations Convention on the Recognition and Enforcement of Foreign Arbitral Awards (New York, 10 June 1958), the decisions of arbitration courts must be recognized and enforced in the territory of foreign states.

As an international court, the ICAS can deal with the following disputes:

- disputes concerning contractual relations arising from the economic activity between two or more companies, of which at least one is foreign;
- disputes between companies created on the RF territory with foreign investments, disputes between international organizations and between international organizations with RF legal subject(s).

The rules on sports arbitration are more clearly defined in Annex N. 5 to the Decree of the Russian Chamber of Commerce and industry N. 6, 11 January 2017 (hereinafter: Sports Arbitration Regulations). Under these rgulations, disputes relating to the following matters in professional and high performance sport may be referred to the ICAS (Article 1(2)):

- admission to sport competitions;
- breach of anti-doping rules;
- sports sanctions;
- the conclusion, change, execution or termination of the contracts among those taking part in sport;
- membership of the All-Russian sport federations and professional sports leagues;
- the status of sportsmen and women and changes of affiliation to clubs/sports organization;
- the powers of the sports event organizers;
- rights and obligations of members of sports teams of the RF and subjects of the RF;
- delegation of sports competition rights;
- disputes between sports agents.

The Federal Law of 22 November 2016 N. 396-FZ On the amendments to the Law on Sport (Law 329-FZ 2007) introduced into the Law on Sport a new Chapter 5.1. (On disputes resolution in professional and high performance sport, Article 36.2. –

74. Provision of the Ministry of Justice N. 109-p of Russian Ministry of Justice.
75. Apart from ICAS, only a Maritime Arbitration Commission at the Chamber of Commerce and Industry of the Russian Federation is exempt from the requirement to obtain government authorization.

36.5.). Pursuant to this law, the permanent arbitration body for disputes in professional and high-performance sport is set up with the participation of the Russian Olympic and Paralympic Committee, and the All Russian sport federations for the sports included in the programme of Olympic/Paralympic games and professional sports leagues (Article 36(2)(paragraph 2))

The parties can refer disputes to arbitration only on condition that an arbitration agreement or arbitration clause is concluded in writing. In relation to the ICAS, as an alternative to the arbitration agreement, an appellate arbitration agreement can be concluded. An appellate agreement is an agreement on the recourse to arbitration in cases in which the claimant does not agree with the decisions of the All-Russian anti-doping organization or sports federations/clubs/leagues (Article 2, regulations on Sports Arbitration).

According to Article 36(2)(paragraph4) of the Law on Sport, an arbitration agreement is deemed to be stipulated if it is included in the regulations approved by the All-Russian Sports Federation or professional sport league, in the regulations of sports competitions with the participation of the federation/league, in the statutes of the All-Russian sports federations or professional sport leagues, and if there is a formal written statement by these subjects (federations, leagues) to testify their intention to comply with the arbitration agreement/clause.

The regular courts are required to uphold the claim subject to arbitration without further examination unless the arbitration agreement is invalid, it is no longer in force, or cannot be executed or is otherwise regulated by federal law.

An authorized permanent arbitration body can carry out the following activities (provided they are specified in its regulations):

- administration of the international commercial arbitration;
- administration of internal disputes;
- separate functions on arbitration administration including the nomination of arbitrators and dismissal of arbitrators in the case of *ad hoc* arbitrations.

II. Arbitrators

116. Federal Law N. 382-FZ, 2015, (Article 47), established stricter requirements in relation to arbitrators. Under its provisions, each permanent arbitration body is required to post on its website a list of recommended arbitrators with no less than 30 persons. At least one-third of them must have a scientific degree awarded on the RF territory and at least 50% must have ten years' experience in civil law disputes resolution as arbitrators or court judges. The same person cannot be included in the lists of the recommended arbitrators of more than three permanent arbitration bodies. Moreover, pursuant to Article 36.2.(paragraph 7) of the Law on Sport, no less than one-half of the arbitrators must possess at least five years' experience in professional and high-performance sport (as coaches, sportsmen or women, or sports judges) before the date of inclusion in the list of recommended arbitrators.

The permanent arbitration body is required to take all the decisions concerning nomination or withdrawal of the arbitrators on a collegial basis through the Committee on Nominations. In cases in which a permanent arbitration body grants such a competence to a single person, the parties must be granted the right to appeal such a decision to the Committee on Nominations.

Two-thirds of the Committee on Nominations are required to be persons included on the recommended list of arbitrators at the permanent arbitration body. Decisions are taken by a simple majority of votes among the persons included on the list. The regulations of the permanent arbitration body may establish a different procedure for the composition of one-third of the Committee on Nominations and additional requirements for its members. The Committee on Nominations is subject to the obligatory rotation of its members: over a period of three years no less than one-third of the members are required to be changed and the same person cannot become a member again within three years of being replaced.

Non-commercial organization under which auspices a permanent arbitration body is created, is required to disseminate information on its bodies and founding members (organizations with more than 100 founding members are exempt from this obligation).

Pursuant to Article 10 of Law N. 382-FZ, 2015 the parties can decide on the number of arbitrators, and, unless otherwise specified in the federal law, the number is required to be odd. If the parties do not agree on the number, as a rule three arbitrators are nominated.

In the case of arbitration with a single arbitrator, if the parties do not agree on the arbitrator, he or she can be appointed by the competent court.

In the case of arbitration with the appointment of a single arbitrator, he/she is required to meet one of the following criteria:

- an advanced-level law degree awarded on the RF territory;
- an advanced-level law degree as attested by the documents of foreign states recognized by the RF.

In case of a collegial hearing, the chair of the arbitration panel is normally required to meet the same criteria. However, the parties may agree that the chair of the panel shall be exempt from these requirements but in this case at least one of the panel members is required to satisfy them.

In the case of an arbitration panel with three arbitrators, the parties are required to inform the ICAS about the arbitrators appointed. In cases in which they are unable to choose them, the arbitrators are nominated by the Committee on Nominations from the lists of recommended arbitrators.

In cases in which the aggregate amount of the claim does not exceed RUB 500,000, the case is normally heard by a single arbitrator appointed by the ICAS President or Vice President from the recommended list of arbitrators on sports disputes (Article 13 of Sport Arbitration Regulations).

The arbitrator cannot be below the age of 25, nor have an outstanding conviction, nor be deprived of a legal capacity (or have limited legal capacity). Moreover, an arbitrator cannot be a person whose professional activity as a judge, lawyer, notary, investigator, prosecutor or similar was terminated in the RF for actions incompatible with his or her professional activity. A further impediment arises when federal law does not allow the nomination of an individual as an arbitrator due to his or her status.

III. Disputes Subject to Arbitration in Professional and High-performance Sport

117. Article 36.3. of the Law on Sport lays down that disputes on the following matters may be referred to arbitration:

- admission to sports competitions;
- breach of anti-doping rules;
- sports sanctions;
- conclusion, change, execution or termination of the contracts among the subjects of sport;
- membership of the All-Russian sports federations and professional sports leagues;
- the status of sportsmen and women and changes in their affiliation to clubs/sports organizations;
- the powers of sports event organizers;
- the rights and obligations of members of sports teams of the RF and subjects of the RF;
- the delegation of sports competition rights;
- disputes between sports agents;
- employment disputes concerning sportsmen and women and coaches in professional and high-performance sport;
- disputes between professional sports leagues and All-Russian Sport Federation on matters of joint competence (as indicated in the Law on Sport, Article 19.2.);
- other disputes between the subjects of physical culture, professional and high-performance sport.

Disputes relating to sports training and disputes not contemplated in this article cannot be subject to arbitration by the permanent arbitration body.

One important innovation is that employment disputes in professional sport are now subject to arbitration. In the previous version of the arbitration law and pursuant to the Civil Code of Practice of the Russian Federation, they were excluded from the competence of the arbitration courts and such cases could be heard only by the regular courts.

Under Article 36.2 (7), the All-Russian sport federations and professional sports leagues are required to impose sanctions on those taking part in sport, including professional and high-performance sport who fail to comply with the award of the arbitration panel, and in any way to provide necessary assistance when the cases of non-compliance with such awards are verified.

. This rule is extended also to the arbitration awards of foreign arbitration bodies recognized by the RF (Article 36.4 (3) of the Law on Sport.

According to international commercial arbitration law, sports arbitration deals with cases based on the law specified by the parties in the agreement and, in the absence of such a provision, on the basis of the law on sports arbitration pursuant to the dispute rules considered most appropriate. Any reference to a foreign law must be considered as referring to the material norms of this law, and not to the rules on conflict-of-laws. The CAS takes a decision on the basis of the terms of the agreement and commercial practice applicable to the specific case (Article 31, Law N. 382-FZ, 2015).

Unless otherwise agreed by the parties or established in federal law, arbitration is confidential and the hearings are held behind closed doors. The arbitrator cannot be called on to give evidence on the facts of which he or she became aware during arbitration.

The parties can participate in the arbitration hearings directly or they may delegate representatives. Failure to appear on the part of the duly informed party is not an impediment to the arbitration procedure (except for justified reasons). Parties to the arbitration can request that the case be heard in their absence. At the request of the parties, videoconferencing can be used during the arbitration. Unless otherwise agreed by the parties, arbitration hearings are not recorded.

As a rule, the arbitration ruling is deemed to be final with no right to appeal to the regular court. Pursuant to Article 421 of the Civil Code of Practice (with the amendments introduced by Law N 409-FZ of 29 December 2015), the arbitration ruling can be annulled in cases in which the claimant party relies on the following circumstances:

- one of the parties to the arbitration agreement lacked full legal capacity;
- the arbitration agreement was invalid pursuant to the law selected by the parties or (if the parties did not agree on the law applied), pursuant to the RF law;
- the party against which the award was issued was not duly notified about the appointment of the arbitrators or the arbitration hearing (the time and place of the hearing) or was unable to give evidence to the arbitration panel for objective reasons;
- the arbitration ruling was issued on a matter beyond the jurisdiction of the arbitration court or beyond its competence. Regular courts can partially annul an arbitration ruling in relation to questions beyond its competence;
- the composition of the arbitration panel or the procedures were contrary to the arbitration agreement or federal law.

The court has the power to annul the arbitration award if:

- the dispute cannot be subject to arbitration according to the RF laws;
- the decision of the arbitration panel is contrary to public order in the RF. In this case a partial annulment can be determined if only one section of the agreement is found to be contrary to public order;
- the decision of the ICAS can be annulled on the basis of international treaties of the RF and Law N. 5338-1 of 7.07.1993 On International Commercial Arbitration;

Termination of arbitration

118. The arbitration procedure can be terminated in cases in which:

- the claimant withdraws the claim and the respondent does not request arbitration within five days of the notification;
- an amicable agreement to terminate the arbitration has been reached;
- the arbitration panel rules that it is not competent to hear the dispute;
- a valid regular court ruling or arbitration ruling has already been issued on the same matter between the parties;
- the prerequisites for arbitration are lacking (for instance, when the claimant fails to take action in this regard for more than three months).

Terms

119. The ICAS or other arbitration court is required to take a decision in a reasonably short period, normally within sixty days of the setting up of the arbitration panel or appointment of a single arbitrator (Article 29, regulations on Sports Arbitration). Either party, upon notification to the other party, has the right within thirty days of the arbitration ruling to request an additional award in relation to matters not dealt with in the final arbitration award. The arbitration court is required to take a decision in this regard within thirty days.

Expenses

120. Pursuant to Article 10 of the Sports Arbitration Regulations, before the initiation of proceedings, the claimant is required to pay registration, arbitration and appellate fees. In the case of a claim for interim measures, the claimant is required to pay an interim fee. The amount is specified in the decree on arbitration expenses.

Pursuant to the Civil Code of Practice of the Russian Federation and Law N. 382-FZ, 2015 (Article 38), the execution of such rulings is mandatory and they are required to be executed voluntarily by the parties to the arbitration agreement. The parties and the arbitration panel are required to ensure that the arbitration award is executable.

Pursuant to Article 41 of Law N. 382-FZ, 2015, if a ruling of the arbitration court is not executed voluntarily and in a timely manner (immediately unless a special term is established in the award), it can be enforced by means of compulsory execution. In order to achieve this outcome, the party in whose favour the ruling has been handed down needs to appeal to the competent court to obtain a receiving order.

IV. Mediation

121. Pursuant to Article 36.5. on pretrial dispute resolution in professional and high performance sport of the Law on Sport, the All-Russian Sport Federation or league can establish an obligatory pretrial dispute resolution for those taking part in the sport.

For this purpose it is allowed to make use of a mediation procedure in accordance with Russian legislation.

Mediation is a relatively new dispute resolution procedure in Russia. The increasing recognition of alternative forms of dispute resolution including mediation resulted in the adoption of a special Law of 27 July 2010 N. 193-FZ On Alternative Dispute Settlement Procedures with the Participation of Mediators (hereinafter: Law on Mediation) and another Federal Law N. 194-FZ of 27 July 2010 On amendments of some legal acts of the RF in relation to the adoption of the Law on Mediation. Both laws entered into force on 1 January 2011. These laws are aimed at the further development of the system of alternative dispute resolution and the reduction of the workload of the regular courts. Law N. 193-FZ, 2010 defines mediation, its scope, the procedural issues for the conclusion of a mediation agreement and professional requirements for mediators and mediation activity.

Pursuant to this legislation, mediation is a voluntary procedure, adopted by the parties with the aim of reaching a mutual agreement (Article 2 of the law). It is aimed at a confidential and constructive approach to solve the problem with the assistance of the mediator. Mediators are required to be independent and their attitude to the parties should be neutral as they act not as judges but as consultants and intermediaries. The parties are free to choose the place, time, territory and terms of the mediation. The principles of mediation such as its voluntary nature, confidentiality, collaboration and equality of the parties as well as impartiality and independency of the mediator are specified in Article 3 of the Law on Mediation.

If the parties conclude an agreement on a mediation procedure (mediation agreement) and agree for a certain period of time not to refer the dispute to the ordinary courts or an arbitration panel for the purposes of regulating the dispute (which has already arisen or may arise in the future), the court is required to recognise the validity of such an agreement except in cases when the party needs to defend its rights (Article 4(1) of the Law on Mediation). The mediation agreement is required to be in writing (Article 7 and 12) and the agreement should specify the following:

- the matter of the dispute;
- the mediator(s) or mediation organization;
- the mediation procedure;
- the terms of the parties' participation and relative expenses;
- the timeframe of the mediation procedure.

The activity of a mediator (mediators) can be carried out free of charge or for remuneration. Mediation organizations should be paid for their services. In either case the amount of the remuneration should be equally divided between the parties (Article 10 of the Law on Mediation).

The terms of the mediation are defined in the agreement but the parties are required to undertake every effort to conclude the procedure within 60 days (Article 13). In exceptional cases the time limit may be extended to a maximum 180 days except in cases when the mediation is carried out after the case has been referred to the regular court or arbitration panel where the established time limit for the hearing is 60 days.

However, not all disputes can be settled by means of mediation or other alternative dispute resolution procedures. For example, such procedures are not permitted in relation to the use of doping or claims against disciplinary sanctions imposed on sportsmen or women. Moreover, such procedures cannot be adopted with regard to collective labour relations or disputes concerning the rights and legitimate interests of third parties who do not participate in the mediation procedure. Rather, such procedures may be adopted in the regulation of disputes relating to discrimination, violation of property rights, violation of broadcasting rights, compensation for injuries and other disputes relating to employment disputes between sportsmen or women and federations, or between federations and clubs.

Mediation can be adopted before a dispute arises or at a subsequent stage when a case in the ordinary or arbitration court has already been initiated (Article 7(2) of the Law on Mediation). There is no impediment to mediation even when a case is under examination in a regular or arbitration court. Law N. 382-FZ of 2015, Chapter 10, Article 49, specifies the relationship between mediation and arbitration. It states that mediation can be used at any stage of the arbitration procedure. In this case the parties must submit to the arbitration panel a written agreement on mediation in accordance with the Law on Mediation. The outcome of the mediation reached by the parties and stipulated in writing can be considered by the arbitration panel as a final arbitration decision with the consent of the parties.

It is important to note that mediation can be carried out on a professional or non-professional basis. Non-professional mediators are required to be at least 18 years old, to have legal capacity to act, and not to have a criminal record. Professional mediators are required to be at least 25 years old, to have an advanced-level degree and to have attended special professional courses on mediation. Professional mediation can be requested also for cases that were referred to the courts (arbitration panels) prior to the mediation procedure. It is not considered to be a commercial activity and mediators are free to conduct any other professional activity except being employed as public officers (Article 15 of the Law on Mediation).

In order to ensure the high professional quality of mediation, government Decree N. 969 of 3 December 2010 establishes a programme of professional training for mediators.

Moreover, Federal Law 194-FZ, 2010 introduced Article 30[1] into the Federal Law on Advertising entitled advertising of mediators' activity in relation of the mediation procedure, prohibiting advertising by mediators who not have an official training certificate issued by the qualified institutions. Any advertising must contain details about such certificates. It is not permitted for advertising by mediators to make claims about the advantages of mediation over regular court or arbitration procedures.

V. Alternative Dispute Resolution Procedure with the Participation of an Intermediary

122. This is a procedure of a voluntary dispute resolution with the participation of a neutral person (intermediary) who is required to assist the parties in reaching agreement.

This procedure is regulated by the conciliation regulation of ICAS entering into force on 1 June 2001.

Any party wishing to adopt this procedure is required to submit an application to the ICAS.

The application must contain the following information:

- names and addresses of the parties;
- short description of the reasons for the dispute;
- amount of compensation requested;
- copy of the consent of the parties to adopt a conciliation procedure, where available;
- signature of the authorized person.

The ICAS is required to inform the other party about the receipt of the application and to issue an opinion about the dispute within fifteen days. In the case in which one of the parties does not consent to the procedure, the claimant can request the ICAS to propose another party to carry out the conciliation procedure. The ICAS contacts another party and requests notification of consent or dissent within thirty days. In the case of a negative response or no response at all the procedure will not be carried out.

In cases in which both parties consent to conciliation, the ICAS nominates an intermediary, unless otherwise agreed by the parties. The intermediary is nominated by the ICAS, its President or Vice President, while questions about termination of its activity are decided by the governing body of the ICAS. Intermediaries are not the parties' representatives and their role consists in assisting the parties to reach an agreement based on principles of objectiveness, bona fides and fairness, with due consideration for the rights and obligations of the parties, customary procedures and the circumstances of the case as well as standard business practice. If an intermediary is involved in circumstances that call into question his impartiality and fairness, he must immediately refer the matter to the ICAS which will take a decision on the activity of the intermediary.

The ICAS provides organizational assistance for the conciliation procedure by:

- forwarding documents to the parties and the intermediary;
- providing assistance in organizing the meeting (determining the date, time and place) and notification;
- providing premises for the meetings;
- receiving advance payment for the procedure and its management, and any other kinds of assistance.

The parties can participate in the meetings themselves or delegate their representatives.

In cases in which the parties reach an amicable agreement, they sign it and it becomes binding.

The intermediary and the parties are required to keep all information confidential, including information on the provisions of the amicable agreement, except in cases when disclosure is necessary for its compulsory performance.

The parties undertake not to disclose the following information during court or arbitration procedures (regardless of whether it concerns the dispute with the intermediary):

- opinions or proposals provided by one of the parties in relation to the dispute;
- the proposals of the intermediary;
- any confession made by one of the parties during the conciliation procedure;
- information about whether a party was ready to accept the intermediary's proposal.

Unless the parties have agreed otherwise, the intermediary cannot act as an arbitrator in any arbitration proceeding in relation to the dispute subject to conciliation. In cases in which an amicable agreement is reached, the parties may agree, with the intermediary's consent, that he will be nominated as an arbitrator and ask him to formalize an amicable agreement as an arbitration award.

The intermediary cannot represent either party during court or arbitration hearings in relation to the dispute for which he was appointed as an intermediary. The parties agree that they will not call an intermediary as a witness in such hearings.

The claimant submitting the application for a conciliation procedure to the ICAS is required to pay a fixed sum of USD 200 as the registration fee, without which the conciliation will not start. The registration fee is non-returnable.

Furthermore, a conciliation fee is required to cover the expenses of the nomination of the intermediary and for other organizational expenses. This normally corresponds to one-third of the corresponding arbitration fee. It must be paid by the parties within thirty days of notification by the ICAS. Unless parties have otherwise agreed, the amount is shared equally by the parties. The conciliation procedure will not start until payment has been made, and in the case of non-payment for more than sixty days the ICAS can terminate the procedure.

§2. Jurisdictional Bodies in Football

123. Under Article 36.5. of the Law on Sport, pretrial dispute resolution in professional and high performance sport, for the purposes of pretrial dispute resolution, the All-Russian sports federations and professional leagues can set up special bodies within their own organizations competent to resolve the disputes referred to in Article 36.3. of the Law on Sport with the possibility to appeal against decisions in the permanent arbitration panel pursuant to Article 36.2. of the Law on Sport and to the arbitration agreement of the federation or league.

In this connection the International Federation of Association Football (FIFA) and the Football Union of Russia (FUR) promote out-of-court dispute resolution pursuant to the regulations on Dispute Resolution[76] (hereinafter: regulations) through the following bodies:

- the Dispute Resolution Chamber;
- the Committee on the Status of Players.

The activity of these two bodies is regulated by the Constitution of the RF, constitutional federal laws, federal laws, normative acts of the RF President and federal government, normative acts of the subjects of RF, international treaties, the FUR Statute and other

76. Latest version: March 2017, N. 166/10.

norms, norms of FIFA, UEFA, customs and other norms in compliance with RF legislation. In cases in which relations are not directly governed by the FUR Regulations, the FIFA Statute and regulations are applied by analogy (Article 1 of the regulations).

I. Dispute Resolution Chamber

124. The Dispute Resolution Chamber is a jurisdictional body of the FUR, responsible for pretrial dispute resolution between football clubs, football players, coaches, agents and other parties pursuant to the FUR Statute. It imposes disciplinary sanctions for the violation of the Regulation on the Status and Transfer of Players and other regulations as specified. Disputes may be referred to the Chamber by clubs, football players, coaches, agents or other parties in football according to the Regulation on the Status and Transfer of Players. The parties to a dispute are not entitled to refer the dispute to the Chamber in cases in which they have already referred it to a regular court, court of arbitration, Dispute Resolution Chamber, the Committee on the Status of Players at FIFA, or the CAS in Lausanne.

The procedure is based on principles of legality, confidentiality, independence, impartiality, competitiveness, equality and equal representation of the parties. The Chamber consists of a president and vice president, ten representatives of professional football players (recommended by the players' trade union pursuant to clause 8 of the regulations on Dispute Resolution) and ten representatives of professional football clubs, recommended by the league under Article 8 of the regulations. The composition of the Chamber is approved by the Executive Committee of FUR for a period of four years. Members of the Chamber are required to have Russian citizenship, and they cannot at the same time be members of the Executive Committee, or the Committee on the Status of Players, or directors of one of the leagues.[77] The president is required to have a law degree.

The seats for professional football club representatives are distributed as follows:

- five seats for the representatives of professional football clubs belonging to the Russian Premier Football League;
- two seats for the representatives of professional football clubs of the National Football League;
- one seat for a representative of five-a-side football;
- one seat for a representative of women's football.

These representatives are nominated by decision of the higher executive body of the league concerned or by consent of the FUR President following collegiate management.

Representatives of professional football players are appointed by the higher body of the association of trade unions, registered as legal persons in the RF territory in compliance with one of the following conditions:

77. Under these regulations directors of the leagues of FUR are persons who, pursuant to the Statute of the FUR or league concerned, can represent the organization without power of attorney.

- membership of an association such as an All Russia trade union or a trade union recognized by Fédération Internationale des Associations de Footballeurs Professionnels (FIFPRO);
- recognition by FIFPRO of such an association.

The Chamber can initiate its activity after approval by half of the established number of representatives.

If more than 30% of the Chamber's rulings are overturned by the Committee or by the CAS over a period of twelve consecutive months, the FUR President places on the agenda of the FUR Executive Committee a request for the Chamber to report on its activity and a motion to change of its composition.

With regard to the powers of the Chamber, it can deal with the following categories of disputes:

- violation of the terms of registration of players, unless referred to the Committee on the Status of Players;
- violation of the norms governing employment contacts between clubs and players;
- violation of an employment contract during the temporary leasing of a player, or violation of supplementary contractual terms or terms on termination of employment contract or violation of collective agreements or other normative acts;
- violation of the terms of the employment contract with coaches admitted to competitions;
- violation of training fees;
- violation of contract terms and compulsory payment in case of contract termination without justified reason, or in the case of the termination by club because of disciplinary violations foreseen in the Russian labour legislation;
- violation of the procedure for the player's release for taking part in competitions as a member of the national team;
- violation of the principles of stability of employment relations in football;
- violation of solidarity rules;
- violation of the terms of transfer contracts (compensation);
- violation of the terms of contracts with football intermediaries and other disputes referred to the Chamber by the FUR for a ruling.

II. Committee on the Status of Players

125. This Committee consists of a president, vice president and ordinary members. The total number of members cannot be more than nine. The previous regulations contemplated the participation of four members from the clubs and four from among the players. The current regulations establish only a general numerical requirement without any specific quotas for the members.

The list of members of the Committee including the president and vice president is determined by the FUR President taking account of the opinion of the professional football clubs and leagues.[78]

The composition of the Committee is approved by the Executive Committee of the FUR for a period of four years. The members of the Committee including the president and vice president are required to have a law degree[79] and Russian citizenship, and the president and vice president must have at least five years' experience of work in the world of football. Members cannot at the same time be members of the Executive Committee, the Chamber, or directors of one of the leagues.

The quorum for the decision-making is four members, one of whom should be the president or vice president.

The current regulations (2016–2017) exclude from its competence a number of important matters relating to the employment disputes between clubs, coaches and players. The following matters are no longer within the competence of the Committee:

- violation of the conclusion of employment contracts between the players and the club;
- violation of the terms of the employment contract during a temporary transfer, and the violation of annexes, additional contract agreements, termination agreements and collective agreements, contracts;
- violation of the terms of employment contract with coaches;
- violation of the terms of obligatory payments in the case of voluntary contract termination without objective reasons or in the case of termination by the club due to disciplinary breaches;
- violation of the stability of employment relations in football.

Disputes concerning transfer contracts and training compensation can be appealed to the Committee.

Under Article 14(2) of the regulations, the Committee is a jurisdictional body of the first instance in relation to claims in relation to:

- the definition of the player's status (professional or amateur);
- claims about legionnaire status;
- claims about the player's registration for taking part in competitions outside the registration period;
- claims concerning the order and terms of registration or inclusion of sportsmen and women, and coaches, on the entry list for participation in competitions, registration of transfer contracts and employment contracts with players/coaches.
- claims on decisions by the regional football federations concerning the definition of the status of the football player as an amateur or professional, violation of registration terms and/or inclusion in the competition entry list.

79. In the previous regulations only the president was required to have a law degree.

Under Article 14(1) of the regulations, the Committee is a jurisdictional body of second instance dealing with claims concerning the rulings of the Chamber on matters within its competence including:

- violation of the terms of payment of training compensation for players;
- violation of the procedure for releasing the player for the purposes of playing for national teams during competitions;
- violation of solidarity rules;
- violation of the terms of transfer contracts (compensation);
- violation of the procedure for the stipulation of transfer contracts (contracts on compensation);
- violation of contracts with intermediaries;
- other disputes within the Chamber's competence and related procedural matters.

The Chamber's decision on these matters can be appealed only to the Committee within five working days of receipt of the final full decision (Article 53(1)) of the regulations.

Under Article 53(2) the Chamber's decision on the following matters can be appealed only to the CAS within twenty-one days of receipt of the final full decision:

- violation of the conclusion of employment contract between the players and the club;
- violation of the employment contract during a temporary transfer period, and violation of annexes, additional contract agreements, termination agreements and breach of collective agreements and contracts;
- violation of the terms of the employment contract with coaches;
- violation of the terms of obligatory payments in the case of a voluntary termination of contract without objective reasons, or in the case of termination by the club due to a breach of discipline;
- violation of the stability of employment relations in football.

This amendment can have negative consequences for players who no longer have the right to appeal to the Committee and have to appeal directly to the CAS which is a costly procedure.

Under Article 20 of the regulations, all the parties are required to take part in the Chamber or Committee hearing or send their delegates. In the case of a more than a one-time violation of this obligation the party may be sanctioned with a fine of up to RUB 80,000. Clubs are further subject to additional coefficients (Article 49(8) 1.0% for the highest division, 0.5% for the first division and 0.25% for all other divisions).

Unlike the previous version of the regulations, the non-appearance of the duly informed party at the Chamber or Committee hearing no longer constitutes an impediment to the hearing (Article 58 of the regulations).

Decisions of the Chamber and Committee are required to be implemented by the parties on a voluntary basis within fourteen working days of their entry into force (unless a different term is established by the Chamber or Committee). Failure to execute the decisions results in the application of the following sanctions:

- in the case of the first delay and first warning: RUB 100,000 for the club and RUB 50,000 for the player/coach;
- in cases in which thirty days have elapsed from the time of the first decision on the failure to implement the decision and the second claim: RUB 500,000 for the club and 100,000 for the player/coach;
- in cases in which thirty days have elapsed from the time of the second decision on the failure to implement the decision and third claim: RUB 1,000,000 for the club and 200,000 for the player/coach;
- in the case of a delay of more than six months and further to other claims against the club: a penalty of three tournament points and for the player/coach, disqualification for four months from competitions under the aegis of the FUR. These sanctions may be repeated in the case of a delay in relation to the newly established term.

The financial sanction may be increased for each failure but by no more than 50%. These sanctions may be repeated in the case of a delay in relation to the newly established term.

Under Article 64 of the regulations, the decisions of the Chamber and Committee can be re-examined in cases in which freshly appeared or fresh evidence comes to light.

Freshly appeared evidence is an evidence essential in cases in which the evidence was unknown to the claimant and existed at the moment of the decision. Further cases include knowingly false witness testimony or knowingly false expert witness testimony, knowingly false translation and falsification of documentation leading to an illegal or improper decision.

Fresh evidence refers to circumstances arising after the decision was taken but relevant for the correct decision on the case (for instance, the recognition of an agreement as illicit by a regular court or an arbitration court) influencing the final decision.

Claims concerning the re-examination of decisions of the Chamber or Committee based on freshly appeared evidence or new circumstances may be filed within three months of such circumstances coming to light. The decisions must be re-examined by the jurisdictional body originally taking the decision. Committee decisions overturning decisions by the Chamber should be taken by the Committee.

The official language of the proceedings is Russian. If one of the parties concerned is not proficient in Russian, an interpreter must be made available. All information must be kept confidential.

Between April 2010 and March 2011 the Chamber dealt with 223 disputes referred by football players, clubs and agents, including 179 referred by players and coaches, 38 by clubs and 6 by agents. It is evident from these figures that the majority of disputes are referred to the Chamber by players. The Committee on the Status of Players overruled only five decisions, whereas two decisions were set aside and replaced with an order for compensation.[80] The main aim of the Chamber is to reconcile the parties and resolve disputes in the pretrial phase while seeking a mutually acceptable

80. CAS 2010/A/2204.

settlement. The percentage of appeals to other courts against the rulings of the Chamber is fairly low.[81]

81. K. N. Gusov, *Activity on the Dispute Resolution Chamber of the Football Union of Russia*, materials of the *V* International Conference on Sports Law: Prospects for Development, Moscow, 2011 (in Russian). (К. Н. Гусов, *Деятельность палаты по разрешению споров российского футбольного союза*, материалы *V* международной научно-практической конференции Спортивное право: перспективы развития М., 2011).

Chapter 3. Taxation

126. Article 57 of the Russian Constitution establishes a common for all citizens obligation to pay taxes. Like many other countries in order to stimulate the development of sport, Russian Tax Code (TC) establishes a series of fiscal benefits in the sphere of professional sport which concern in particular sportsmen with disabilities and associations where such people represent a determined threshold. Moreover certain activities in relation to the organization and holding of large-scale sport events like Olympiads and World Cups may benefit from tax relief.

§1. Value Added Tax (VAT)

127. In Russia VAT was first time introduced in 1992[82] and its regulation has been subject to numerous changes since then. Actually VAT is regulated by the Chapter 21 of the Tax Code.

128. VAT has to be paid by the following subjects:

(a) organizations;
(b) individual entrepreneurs;
(c) persons who must pay it because of the transportation of goods beyond the customs border of the Customs Union according to the customs legislation in force.

129. The following foreign actors are exempt from VAT if they are:

(1) foreign organizers of XXII Olympic games and XI Paralympics games of Sochi 2014[83] (according to Article 3 of the 'Olympic law') or foreign commercial partners of the International Olympic Committee in relation to the organization of Olympic and Paralympics games in Sochi 2014 official sponsors, suppliers, licensees and official mass media within the framework of the organization of the Olympic games).
(2) organizations of the official broadcasters of the Sochi 2014 Olympic games in relation to the operations regarding spread of mass media information concerning the games during the period of the Olympic games[84] (Article 3.1. of the Olympic law).

82. Disposition of Supreme Council RSFSR of 6 Dec. 1991 N 1994-I on the modality of enactment of the laws of RSFSR 'on the VAT law' and 'Excise duty law', Alekseyev, *supra* n. 17, 2012, 560.
83. Foreign organizers of Sochi 2014 Olympic games are IOC, International Paralympic Committee and organizations which are under control of these bodies or in which activity they take part as specified by the Government of the RF. The list of marketing partners of IOC and official broadcasting companies is approved by the RF Government (Art. 3(1) Olympic Law).
84. The period of Olympic games is considered a period including one month before the opening ceremony, the whole period of the Olympic and Paralympics games and one month after the closing ceremony of Paralympics (Art. 2(2) of the Olympic law).

130. According to the Article 148(1) TC RF, VAT is subject to be paid for the services provided on the territory of the RF in the sphere of physical culture, sport, tourism and recreation. However, on some occasions it can be possible to benefit from tax relief in the sphere of sport.[85] In particular the exemptions concern the activities of the Russian commercial partners of the IOC acting in relation to the organization of the Olympic games of 2014 on the territory of the RF.

131. Moreover Article 149(3) TC RF exempts the activity of physical culture organizations linked to the sale of the entrance tickets[86] for the sport events organized by them and for the services linked to the leasing of sport buildings for these events. In the meantime, the sale of the radio and television rights linked to the sport events are subject to VAT.

132. The organizations unifying sportsmen with disabilities may benefit from tax relief. According to the Article 149(3) TC RF the following operations are exempt: realization (including delivery, fulfilment, use for own needs) of the products (except products subject to the excise duties, minerals and mineral resources and other goods) works and services (except of brokerage and other intermediary services) performed by the following organizations:

- public organizations of disabled persons where disabled sportsmen and their legitimate representatives constitute not less than 80%
- organizations whose full charter capital consists of the deposits of the public organizations of disabled, where people with disabilities constitute at least 50% of their total workforce and the share of their salary in the overall company salary capital is no less than 25%
- organizations whose exclusive owners are organizations of disable persons created for educational, cultural, scientific, curative or other social purposes as well as for the purpose of help to disable people, disable children and their parents.

133. According to the Article 150(1) import in Russian territory of the technical means and materials used only for the prevention of disability and rehabilitation is exempt from VAT.[87]

134. One of the dubious points is whether transfer fees should be subject to VAT.

Some believe that compensation received for this operation cannot be compared to operations like realization of services or goods and thus should not be subject to VAT.[88] Different position was taken in the judgment of the Federal Monopoly service

85. Provision of the RF President from 22 Nov. 1993 n. 1973 'On full support of physical culture and sport'.
86. If the form of the tickets is approved for the blanks of strict accountability as specified in the circular of the Minister of Culture and Sport from 17 Dec. 2008 N. 257 'About the blanks of strict accountability'.
87. Governmental provision from 21 Dec. 2000 N. 998 specifies this means.
88. *See* court decision of the presidium of High Arbitration Court RF N 11967 in reference to case N A65-33687/2005-CA1-19 from 27 Feb. 2007 linked to the transfer of hockey players from one club to other clubs, cited in S. V. Alekseyev, *supra* n. 17, 2012, 566.

(FAS) of Ural Okrug related to the transfers of football players when the operations were subject to VAT.[89] There is still no commonly accepted legal position on this point.

§2. Income Tax

135. Federal Law from 5 August 2000 N. 118-FZ introduced into the Russian Tax Code a special Chapter 23 which became effective from 1 January 2001. Pursuant to Russian tax legislation, income taxpayers are Russian and non-Russian citizens who are recognized as Russian fiscal residents. Foreign people are subject to income tax if their income is received on the RF territory. Russian fiscal residents are persons who reside on the territory of the Russian Federation for more than 183 calendar days within twelve consecutive months. These periods are not interrupted in case of temporary travels (of less than six months) for the purposes of study and medical treatment. Regardless of their physical presence on the RF territory, Russian fiscal residents include Russian military personnel and civil servants posted on overseas missions.

136. The taxable base includes all incomes received by the person in natural and monetary form as well as material profit (Article 212 TC RF). Practical question is if health services provided by employers to their employees like swimming pool, gymnasium, fitness centres) should be taxed. There is no unique position in this regard. The supporters of the first position state that these benefits should be taxed.[90] The second position advocates that these benefits should not be taxed as it is not always possible to personify the amount of each benefit.[91]

137. Some kind of incomes are released from taxation (Article 217 TC RF). They include:

(a) payment of food, sport equipment, sport uniform received for the purposes of training for participation in the competitions;
(b) expenses related to reimbursement of expenses related to the work missions in and out of Russia within the established limits;
(c) prizes in monetary or natural form received by the sportsmen (including disable) for the participation in the competitions as Olympic, Paralympics, Deaf Olympic games, world chess championships (Article 217(20) TC);
(d) payments made by trade unions (included material aid) from the collection of trade union fees (excluded labour related or other kinds of remuneration) as well as payments made by youth organizations to their members from trade union collected fees for organization of mass cultural and sport events (Article 217(31) TC RF);
(e) income of the sportsmen participating in Olympic games 2014 against the Olympic or Paralympics certification and accreditation (Article 217(49) TC RF);

89. *See* decision of FAS (federal antimonopoly service) of Ural Okrug from 23 Aug. 2006 n. Ф09-7230/06-C2, case NA47-15515/05, Alekseyev, *id.* 566.

90. Decision of FAS from 16 Jul. 2010 on case A29-8359/2009, decision of FAS from 19 Apr. 2007 on case A29-3364/2006a, S. V. Alekseyev, *supra* n. 17, 2012, 586.

91. Decision of FAS of Ural Okrug, from 26 Oct. 2006 N Ф09-8909/10-C3 on case A71-19704/2009A24; FAS of Ural Okrug, N Ф09-5950/09-C2 on case N A07-16350-A-ГАР.

(f) incomes of natural persons who are temporary personnel[92] for the period of organization and carrying out the Olympic games of 2014 who concluded labour contracts with the marketing partner of the IOC for the works related to the organization of Olympic games 2014;
(g) incomes in natural form for expenses related to visa or invitations linked to the Sochi 2014 Olympic games and other expenses like interpreting/broadcasting, transporting, souvenirs, etc. for representatives of the international and national Olympic and Paralympics committees, representatives of international and national sport federations, natural persons with Olympic/Paralympics certificate and accreditation, persons who concluded labour contracts with the organizers of Sochi 2014 Olympiad and volunteers.

138. The widespread problem of double taxation for sportsmen working abroad is dealt with on the basis of the bilateral double taxation treaties basing on the two main principles of the international law as *lex domicilii* and *lex rei sitae.*

139. Article 232 TC RF states that the taxes paid abroad by the Russian fiscal residents in relation to the incomes received on the territories of different states and according to their fiscal laws are not considered by fiscal authorities in Russia unless it is established in the bilateral agreements with the foreign states concerned. To be able to benefit from the tax reliefs the tax payer must present to the Russian fiscal agency all the necessary documentation regarding his residence status and taxes paid in another country (with which there is an agreement of avoidance of double taxation) as well as duly certified official fiscal declaration.

§3. Other Taxes

140. There are a number of other taxes applicable to the sport organizations. Among them there is a property tax regulated by Chapter 30 of TC RF.[93] It is a regional tax established at the level of the subjects of the RF which are free to determine the terms and modality of its payment and respective accountability as well as the tax rate within the limits of the Chapter 30 TC RF (anyway not exceeding 2.2%).

141. According to the Article 373 TC RF, the taxpayers are organizations which have taxable (according to the Article 373 TC RF) property, including foreign organizations operating in RF through their permanent representation offices.[94] Under the Article 374 TC RF, movable and immovable property (including temporary property,

92. According to Art. 10.1 of Olympic law, temporary personnel are Russian citizens living abroad and foreign citizens who concluded labour contracts with the marketing partners of the Olympic Committee for the period of Sochi Olympic games 2014.
93. Introduced into the TC from 1 Jan. 2004.
94. For the foreign organizations which do not carry out their activity in the RF through their representation offices the property situated on the RF territory and belonging to foreign organizations or received under concession agreement.

leasing, trust management, for joint activity, or received under a concession agreement) is subject to taxation.[95]

142. Among sport organizations which may benefit from tax relief there are organizers of the Sochi Olympiad 2014 and marketing partners of the IOC (only for the property used for the purposes of the organization of the Olympiad and development of Sochi city as a mountain resort). The other beneficiaries are public organizations of people with disabilities which under the Article 381(3) TC RF, can benefit from property tax relief on condition that the share of disable and/or their legal representatives in the organization is no less than 80% and carried out activity is in line with the Statute. In particular, for All-Russian organizations of people with disabilities tax relief is applied in relation the activity linked to the cultural, health related, scientific, rehabilitation purposes as well as various kind of assistance to people with disabilities, their parents and children. The property used for different purposes is taxed under the general rule and separate accountability is required.

143. The following assets are not taxable:

- plot of the land or natural resources;
- property belonging on the rights of operative management to federal executive bodies which serve for national military or alternative service purposes (like Ministry for Internal Affairs, the Ministry of the Russian Federation for Civil Defence, Emergencies and Elimination of Consequences of Natural Disasters.

144. Tax on profits of the organization is regulated by the Law from 27 December 1991 N. 2116-I and actually is included in the Chapter 25 of the Tax Code which sets forth the procedure and criteria of the definition of profits. Under the Article 245 TC RF the taxpayers are:

- Russian organizations.
- Foreign organizations performing activity in Russia through their permanent branches or/and receiving profits from the activities on the territory of the RF.

145. The reliefs are foreseen for the organizers of the Sochi Olympiad 2014 and marketing partners of the IOC for the profits received in relation to the organization of the Sochi-2014 Olympic games; for official broadcasting organizations in relation to the profits received from mass media production during Sochi 2014 Olympic games and tele- and radio broadcasting services and other channels of mass media production and distribution during the Olympic games (on condition they concluded an agreement with the IOC or its authorized body).

146. Tax relief is foreseen for some kinds of profits such as:

- Profits used for the preparation of citizens on military professions and military training and military patriotic education of youth (for organizations forming part of DOSAAF[96]).

---

95. This property must figure out in the accountable balance as main fixed assets (excluded trustee property and concession agreement property).
96. Voluntary association of assistance to army, aviation and fleet.

- Russian organizers of Sochi 2014 Olympic games in relation to their organization on condition the profit is used for the purposes foreseen by law and statutes for the Russian organizers of Sochi 2014 Olympic games.
- Profits received by the Russian marketing partners of IOC in relation to the fulfilment of their duties (including profits from the sale of the goods and services, property rights, etc.) and so on.

147. Under the Articles 252 and 265 TC RF the taxable base is defined by detracting the expenses (or documented losses) from the profits. Article 270 TC RF specifies which expenses are not calculated in the taxable base. Among them there are expenses of the Russian organizers of the Sochi 2014 Olympic games in relation to this activity and Russian marketing partners of the IOC for the expenses related to the organization of this event and sustained during the period of the event.[97]

148. Land tax is regulated by the Land Registry Code[98] and TC (Chapter 31, Part X, introduced by Federal Law N 141-FZ from 29 November 2004). As in case of property tax, land tax is a regional tax and analogously its regulation is left at the discretion of the subjects of the RF within the limit established by law. Under Article 388 TC taxpayers are legal and natural persons which have property right for the land, or right for its unlimited use. All-Russian organizations of people with disabilities with a share of such people and their representatives of at least 80% can benefit from tax relief under the Article 395(5) TC RF. Moreover legal and natural persons are exempt in case of the use of the land free of charge or in case of leasing.

149. Among other taxes road tax can be mentioned which is obligatory for payment at the territory of the subjects of the RF. It is regulated in the Chapter 28 of the TC RF introduced by the Federal Law from 24 July 2002 N. 110-FZ. As property and land tax, it is regulated by the laws of the subjects within the limits of the Tax Code. Article 357 TC RF establishes the conditions on which it is possible to benefit from tax relief. As in previous cases (Article 358 TC RF) the organizers of Sochi Olympiad and their marketing partners are exempt from this tax in relation to the transportation means registered at their names and used for the purposes of the organization of this event and for the development of Sochi city as a mountain resort.

150. In addition to the above-mentioned tax benefits, Russian tax legislation establishes further fiscal facilitations in relation to the organization of the Sochi 2014 Olympic games. They concern in particular the governmental duty. Under the Article 333.35(3) TC RF the exemptions are established in the following cases:

- for the relevant actions carried out by the Sochi 2014 Organizing Committee in collaboration with the national Olympic and Paralympics committees including actions aimed to protect Olympic an Paralympic symbols
- for a series of other actions in relation to the invitations, visa and other documents for foreign participants in the organization process in relation to the Olympic games.

---

97. Alekseyev, 2012, *supra* n. 17, 566–576. More details on this tax can be found in the Arts 246–333 TC.
98. Art. 7 of the land registry code establishes the principle of the paid use of the land.

151. In the same vein, there are a series of customs duty reliefs contemplated in the law from 21 May 1993 N. 5003-1 'On customs tariff'. Under the Article 35 of this law, the goods (except those subject to excise duties) used for the purposes of the Sochi 2014 Olympic games and on condition of the presentation of the required documentation are exempt from this duty.[99]

99. Governmental provision from 21 Dec. 2009 N 1041 specifies the list of such goods. *See* Alekseyev, 2012, *supra* n. 17, 593–595.

Chapter 4. Private Regulation

152. In Russia there are more than 150 kinds of sport which are specified in the All-Russian register on kinds of sport.[100] The unified All-Russian sport classification establishes the parameters to compare different sports and to award sports titles, categories and qualifications to the sportsmen.[101]

153. Article 22 of the 'Law on Sport' mentions the following sport titles:

- master of sports of the international class
- master of sports of Russia
- grandmaster of Russia

154. The following sports categories:

- candidate to master of sports
- first sports category
- second sports category
- third sports category
- first youth sports category
- second youth sports category
- third youth sports category.

and the following qualification categories for referees:

- sports referee of the All-Russian category
- sports referee of the first category
- sports referee of the second category
- sports referee of the third category
- young sports sport referee.

155. The unified All-Russian sport classification establishes the norms and requirements to be awarded to the corresponding sport titles and categories for the kinds of sport included in the All-Russian register on the kinds of sport and conditions of the performance of these requirements. The provision on the unified All-Russian sport classification determines the contents of these norms and terms and the modality of the award of the titles/qualifications in different kinds of sport. The modality of the award of the qualification categories of the sports referees and their rights and duties are adopted by the federal executive body in physical culture and sport following the applications from the All-Russian sport federations.

156. In Russia the following federations on non-Olympic kinds of sport exist:

- Russian Federation of the Aviation Sports

100. Approved by the circular of the Federal Agency On Physical Culture and sport and tourism from 28 Sept. 2004 N 273, http://www.minsport.gov.ru/sport/high-sport/priznanie-vidov-spor/.
101. Approved by the regulation of Minsport from 21 Nov. 2008 N 48.

- Russian Federation of Sport Acrobatics
- Russian Federation of Baseball
- Russian Federation of Billiards
- Russian Federation of Powerboating
- Russian Federation of Sport Bowling
- Russian Federation of Water-skiing
- Russian Motorcycle Sports Federation
- Russian Federation of Sport Orienteering
- Russian Wushu Federation
- Russian Chess Federation
- Russian Hockey with the Ball Federation
- Russian Rock Climbing federation
- Russian Union of Martial Arts
- All-Russian Federation of Sambo
- Russian Federation of Sumo
- Russian Softball Federation
- All-Russian Squash Federation
- Russian Union of Dance Sport
- Russian Federation of Alpinism
- Russian Federation of Underwater sport.

157. The following federations on winter Olympic sports:

- Russian Biathlon Union
- Russian Bobsleigh Federation
- Russian Alpine Skiing and Snowboarding Federation
- Russian Skating Union
- Curling Federation
- Russian Cross-country Skiing
- Federation of Ski Jumping and Nordic Combined of Russia
- Russian Luge Federation
- The Figure Skating Federation of Russia
- Russian Federation of Freestyle
- Russian Ice Hockey Federation (RIHF).

158. The following federations on summer Olympic sports:

- National Russian Federation of Badminton
- Russian Basketball Federation
- Russian Box Federation
- Russian Wrestling Federation
- Russian Cycling Federation
- Russian Water Polo Federation
- All-Russian Volleyball Federation
- Russian Handball Federation
- Russian Federation of Sport Gymnastics

- All- Russian Federation of free callisthenics
- Russian Federation of Rowing
- Russian Federation of Water Slalom
- All-Russian Federation of Canoe Sprint
- Russian Federation of Judo
- Russian Federation of Horseback Riding
- All-Russian Athletic Federation
- All- Russian Federation of Yachting Sport
- All-Russian Swimming Federation
- Russian Federation of synchronized swimming
- Russian Federation of Water Jumping
- Russian Federation of Trampolining
- Russian Federation of Rugby
- Russian Federation of Modern Pentathlon
- Russian Archery Federation
- Russian Shooting Union
- Russian Tennis Federation
- Russian Table Tennis Federation
- Russian Triathlon Federation
- Russian Taekwondo Union
- Russian Federation of Weightlifting
- Russian Fencing Federation
- Football Union of Russia
- Russian Field Hockey Federation.

159. More information about some sport federations (chosen at random) is as follows.

160. Russian Ice Hockey Federation (RIHF):[102] RIHF was created in 1946 under the direction of the famous football and hockey player Pavel Mihailovich Korotkov.

The Federation is the All-Russian public organization created for the purposes of development and popularization of hockey in Russian Federation. RIHF is the member of the International Ice-Hockey Federation (IIHF) and represents interests of Russian Hockey in international hockey organizations. RIHF carries out its activity on the territory of sixty-seven subjects of the Russian Federation.

161. All hockey competitions on the territory of Russia are held under the umbrella of RIHF. They include Championship of Russia, Russian Championship in the High League, Russian Championship among women teams, Russian Championships in first and second leagues, Russian Championships with the participation of youth teams of the regions and youth club teams.

162. All-Russian National Boxing Federation:[103] Russian Boxing Federation is the All-Russian boxing public organization created on 1 February 1992 after the collapse of the USSR and termination of the activity by the Soviet Boxing Federation. According to its Statute approved on 18 November 2012 the federation is a public organization whose purpose is to promote boxing among Russian people. It operates

102. *See* http://fhr.ru.
103. http://boxing-fbr.ru/.

according to the principles of voluntariness, equal opportunities of its members, transparency and legitimacy. It respects the provisions of the Russian Constitution and other laws, international norms and the norms of the International Boxing Association (AIBA).

163. Cross-Country Skiing Federation of Russia:[104] All-Russian Cross-country skiing federation was created in 1992 and is a public organization. It is a member of the Russian Olympic Committee and has exclusive rights in relation to organization of the ski competitions in Russia and presentation of this kind of sport at the international level. The federation operates in sixty-seven subjects through the accredited regional sport federations, members or structural units of the Federation and through not accredited regional sport units.

164. Russian Volleyball Federation:[105] Officially volleyball was born in Russia on 28 June 1923 when friendly match took place in Moscow between the representatives of the theatre institute and cinema institute. In 1932 an All-Soviet volleyball section was founded and in 1959 All-Soviet Volleyball Federation. In this period it was a really mass sport.

165. All-Russian volleyball federation was founded in 1991 and from 1992 it became official Russian successor of the ex Soviet federation in all international affairs and associations.

166. Russian Basketball Federation:[106] The Russian basketball federation was created on 27 October 1991 and in 1992 was recognized by the FIBA as a successor of the USSR. It unifies basketball associations in seventy subjects of the Russian Federation and represents Russia in the international arena.

167. Russian Biathlon Union:[107] Russian Biathlon Union is an All-Russian public organization created in 1992. It consists of fifty regional representative offices.

168. Russian Chess Federation:[108] Russian chess federation as a successor of the USSR chess federation started its activity from 15 February 1992. It is the All-Russian public voluntary association unifying chess federations of the other subjects of the RF and represents chess sport in the international arena. Its head office is located in Moscow. It is a member of the World Chess Federation (FIDE).

169. Russian Bobsleigh and Skeleton Federation:[109] The Russian Bobsleigh Federation is a voluntary and self-regulatory, All-Russian non-governmental organization established in 1992. The Federation is a member of the All-Russian Union of Physical Culture and Sporting Community Associations 'The Russian Olympic Committee', and the International Bobsleigh and Tobogganing Federation (FIBT). The Federation has different regional divisions, branches and representation offices in various subjects of the Russian Federation.

170. The Figure Skating Federation of Russia:[110] All-Russian Figure Skating Federation was founded in 1992 and is a public organization operating according to

104. http://www.flgr.ru/flgr/history/.
105. http://www.volley.ru/.
106. http://russiabasket.ru.
107. http://biathlonrus.com.
108. http://ruchess.ru/federation/.
109. http://rusbob.ru/en/federation/about.html.
110. http://fsrussia.ru/.

the principles of voluntariness, equal opportunities of the members, legitimacy and transparency.

171. The Football Union of Russia (FUR):[111] The Football Union of Russia is the main football organization in Russia. The RFU is the All–Russia Federation officially recognized by FIFA. The main aims of the FUR are the development and promotion of football in Russia, the management of football events, and the formation of national football teams. The FUR brings together territorial and regional federations, football clubs with the status of public bodies and football academies. It also collaborates with local sports committees in the federal bodies of the RF. The management body of the FUR is a conference which elects the president and Executive Committee for a five-year term of office, and the Executive Committee runs the FUR between conferences. In order to solve problems more effectively, the FUR has a number of departments (sport, finance, international and so on). The governing jurisdictional bodies are as follows:[112]

- Governing and Disciplinary Committee
- Ethics Committee
- Committee on the Status of Players
- Dispute Resolution Chamber
- Commission on agents' activity
- Appeals Committee.

172. The following stakeholders are involved in the Russia football system: the Football Union of Russia (FUR), leagues, federations, football clubs participating in the competitions under the aegis of the FUR, sport academies participating in the competitions under the aegis of the FUR, football players and coaches and football intermediaries.

173. League: a non-commercial partnership,[113] Russian Football Premier League,[114] National Football League,[115] Professional Football League,[116] Association of Mini-Football in Russia[117] or any other body organizing football competitions under the aegis of the FUR and obeying to its rules.

174. Federation: regional football federations and interregional unions of football federations.

175. Association: FIFA member governing football in a certain territory.

176. Professional football club: a football club founded as a legal person and member of the Russian Football Premier League, National Football League and

111. http://www.rfs.ru/.
112. http://www.rfs.ru/rfs/comittees/jurisdictional/.
113. According to Art. 8 of the Federal Law on non-commercial partnerships, of 12 Jun. 1996 N. 7-FZ the non-commercial partnership is a non-commercial organization based on membership, established by natural or/and legal persons to help its members to achieve specific aims under the law (Art. 2(2)).
114. http://www.rfpl.org/.
115. http://1fnl.ru/.
116. http://www.pfl-russia.com/.
117. http://amfr.ru/.

Professional Football League, and recognized by the FUR as participating in professional football competitions.

177. Amateur football club: a club participating in amateur competitions organized by the FUR or the federations.

178. Sports academy: an autonomous legal body or branch of a football club that recognizes the norms of the FUR and whose aim is the training of young football players under the guidance of coaches including practical training and organization of their participation in amateur competitions under the aegis of the FUR.[118]

179. The All-Russian Sports Federations are public state-accredited organizations whose aim is to promote one or more sports, the organization of sporting events and the training of members of sports teams.[119]

118. The definitions are taken from the Regulations on the Status and Transfer of Players (2011), http://www.rfs.ru/rfs/documents/strategies, last amendments from 30 Mar. 2015.
119. Art. 2(6) law 329-FZ of 4 Dec. 2007.

Part II. Sports and Employment

Chapter 1. Legal Regulation of Employment Relationship of Sportsmen

§1. General Legal Issues and Status of the Main Sport Stakeholders

180. As it has been mentioned before the Law 329-FZ 2007 ('Law on Sport') and the Labour Code do not provide any definitions of professional and amateur players and do not provide an exact differentiation of their status as it is done in the regulations of sport federations like FIFA.[120] Russian legal texts rather adopt the term 'professional sport' which is defined as sporting activity aimed at organizing and carrying out sport competitions for which players are remunerated or receive a regular salary provided that this is their main activity (Article 2(11), 'Law on Sport'). Membership of the sports organization is defined on the basis of the existence of an employment contract concluded with this organization (Article 27(3) 'Law on Sport'). As a result all categories (professionals, amateurs, and elite sportsmen and women) are grouped together under the generic term 'sportsmen' defined as physical persons practising a certain sport and taking part in sports events (Article 2, 'Law on Sport'). This means that the definition of professional sports activity can be inferred from factors such as a regular income from sport and an employment contract in written form with a duly established sports body. According to Russian Labour Code (Article 67(1) LC RF) employment contracts must be concluded in written form only. In any case even if not stipulated in written form the contract will be considered concluded by virtue of the fact that the employee started working for the employer with the awareness and consent of the latter. In this case the employer must conclude the contract in a written form within the three days from the beginning of the employment relations.

181. Considering the vagueness of certain norms in the sports legislation, as it has been mentioned, it is logical to expect more precise definitions in the regulations of various kinds of sport. With regard to football, the regulations governing the status and transfer of players contain definitions of professional and amateur players. According

120. Prokopets M., Rogachev D., De Veger F., *Sport disputes resolution*, Moscow, Statute, 2012, 69 (in Russian). (М. Прокопец, Д. Рогачев, Ф. Де Вегер, *Разрешение футбольных споров*, М. Статут,, 2012, 69).

to section 2, Article 3 of the regulations, football players taking part in competitions under the aegis of the FUR may have a professional or an amateur status. Professionals are players who have a written employment contract with a professional football club and who are remunerated for their activity. The amount of this remuneration should be greater than the expenses of the player relating to training and participation in football competitions. In this regard the provisions of the article comply with the FIFA requirements, in particular with the Article 2 of the FIFA Regulations stating in this regard the following: 'a professional is a player who has a written contract with a club and is paid more for his footballing activity than the expenses he effectively incurs. All other players are considered to be amateurs'.

182. Football players who are not professionals are amateurs. Amateur players may receive compensation for the expenses for food, travel, living subsistence, equipment and insurance relating to training for football competitions. Disputes arising from the definition of the status of players are resolved by the Committee on the status of players. Article 4 of the regulations lays down the procedure for the reinstatement of amateur status.

183. In hockey according to the Regulations on the Status and Transfer of Hockey Players from 28 May 2007 registered hockey player may have the following status:

- student of the hockey school
- professional player

184. Basketball player can be either amateur or professional.[121]

185. Sportsmen and women practising mainly individual sports[122] can conclude contracts under the civil law. However, it is not permitted to conclude such contracts to circumvent employee protection legislation. In the presence of factors that are typical of salaried employment, the courts can rule that it is indeed an employment relationship.

I. Legal Status of the Main Sport Stakeholders

186. Employers of professional sportsmen can be legal and natural persons registered as individual entrepreneurs. Natural persons not registered as individual entrepreneurs have no right to be employers.[123] In some cases laid down by federal laws, other bodies may also have the right to conclude employment contracts (Article 20 LC RF).[124] In particular Article 348 LC RF establishes the normative measures

121. Status of basketball player is adopted by the Executive Committee of Russian Basketball Federation from 22 Jul. 2004 amended 4 Aug. 2006 *see* www.basket.ru in K. N., Gusov, O. A., Scevchenko, *Sports law*, Moscow, 2009 (in Russian). (Гусов К. Н., Шевченко О. А. Спортивное право), М. 2009.

122. The legislation does not explicitly prohibit this for collective sports, and it is a common practice for employment contracts to be concluded in these cases.

123. This restriction may be a severe limitation on coaches since in theory physical persons might wish to hire them as personal trainers.

124. According to Civil Code, Art. 55 – they can be branches or representative offices of the companies.

regulating relations between coaches and sportsmen and specifies that these measures must be adopted by the employer in accordance with Article 8 LC RF taking account of the norms laid down by the All-Russian sports federations and the views of the trade union. Article 348(1) states that any lowering of the level of the rights and guarantees of professional sportsmen and coaches as well as any increase in the level of disciplinary or material liability should be carried out only as part of the LC RF.

187. Coach: Legal definition of the coach is contained in the Article 2 of the Law on Sport which defines him as a natural person who has a special vocational or higher professional education and who carries out educational and training activities with sportsmen and conduct their competition activity in order to achieve sport results. In Labour Code (Article 348-1 LC), coaches are defined as natural persons with proper professional qualifications providing training for sportsmen and women, and guiding their competition-related activity to achieve certain results. The activity of the coach is regulated in the local normative acts to a less extent. Normally they regulate the coaching staff in relation to national teams. The activity of coach includes both the pedagogical and sporting treats. The coaches are subject to the procedure of attestation carried out by the sport federations in order to determine their level of qualification.[125] The coaches must confirm their qualification on a three-year basis. In tennis the coaches must have special certificates.[126]

188. Referee: According to Article 2 of the 'Law on Sport' the referee is a natural person authorized by the organizer of sport event to ensure the rules of the game and competition regulation. He must have a special professional qualification. The work of the referee depends on the particular sport. Normally referee is not a profession. They act as volunteers and are not paid, being entitled to the compensation of the expenses in relation to the sport event.

189. On 7 November 2006 the Ministry of Sport[127] adopted a regulation 'On Sport Referees' N. 740. It regulates the modality of qualification and professional requirements for each particular sport. Pursuant to it the following categories of referees exist:

- sport referee of All-Russian category
- sport referee of I category
- sport referee of II category
- sport referee of III category
- sport referee junior.[128]

190. When the category is awarded the referee acquires his referee's book and badge. The profession of sport referee is not mentioned in the Russian professional classification table so special training is ensured at the qualification courses. According to the N. 740 it is required to participate in such courses one time each four years (re-

125. Article 16 of the Law on Sport.
126. Regulation of tennis federation of Russia from 14 Sept. 2016.
127. The then Rossport (federal agency on physical culture and sport) whose functions were transferred to the Ministry of Sport in 2008.
128. Can be awarded to Russian citizens below the age of 16 years.

attestation). They are held in the All-Russian Federations of particular kind of sport or in their departments.

The regulation N. 740 specifies the sanctions for various kinds of misbehaviour or violations. In case of failure to fulfil their obligations referees may be deprived of their qualification category, disqualified or the qualification category may be downgraded. If the disqualification period lasts more than a year, then re-attestation is required.

191. Sport Federation: The definition of sport federation is provided in the Article 2 of the 'Law on Sport' which defines it as a public organization founded in base of the membership with the aim to promote one or more kinds of sport, to manage sporting events and to train members of sports teams. One federation for each kind of sport may be established at the level of the Russian Federation (for All-Russian sport federations) and one for each kind of sport at regional level (at the level of the subject of the RF). The federations must be state-accredited.[129]

II. The Status of Minors

192. Employment of minors is a very important issue in general and in relation to sport in particular because of the higher efforts, risks of injuries and professional diseases and intensiveness of training which might interfere with the duty of general education. Russian labour legislation prohibits to employ minors on works with hazardous or dangerous conditions, limits their working hours and overtime, possibility to employ them on Sundays, holidays or at night work, wages, or to move high weights, limits their dismissals, etc.[130] In relation to sport Article 348(8) of the LC RF establishes the following conditions for workers below the age of 18 years:

- daily working hours may be fixed in collective agreements and local normative acts on condition of observance of the weekly maximum of working hours. Article 92 LC RF provides a reduced working week. For workers below the age of 16 it may not exceed 24 hours per week, for workers between sixteen and eighteen no more than 35 hours per week, for students below the age of 18 half of these established working hours according to age norms;
- the possibility to send them to business missions (trips), employ overtime, at night work, on Saturdays and Sundays and holidays can be established in collective agreements, local normative acts and labour contracts;
- it is allowed to exceed the maximum weighs for manual movements if it is necessary for preparation of minor sportsmen for the competition and their state of health certified by medical doctors permits this;
- it is allowed to conclude employment contract with a sportsman below 14 years only upon the consent of one of the parent or guardianship authority in base of the medical check-up defined by the RF government. The contract must be signed by the parent or minor representative;

129. The modality of accreditation is defined in the regulation of Ministry of Sport from 20 Feb. 2009 N. 49.
130. Chapter 42 LC RF.

- the minors can be temporary transferred to another employer according to Article 348(4) LC RF and employment contract must be concluded on general terms of LC RF accordingly to the age of minor.

§2. Contractual Terms of the Parties According to the Labour Code

193. As mentioned above, the Labour Code of the RF includes a section regulating the working conditions of sportsmen/women and coaches. Pursuant to Article 348.2 LC RF, athletes and coaches can conclude either open-ended or fixed-term contracts for up to five years, in the same way as any other category of workers. Under the Russian legislation it is possible to stipulate fixed-term contract in the cases specified in Article 59 LC RF. Article 59(1) LC RF states that such a contract may be concluded when it is required by the *nature of the work* or its *specific conditions* (temporary substitution of another worker, work abroad, temporary work (for up to two months) and seasonal work, with persons hired for work in organizations located in the regions of the Far North and comparable territories or in emergency situations). Article 59(2) regulates the cases when such a contract is concluded based on the agreement between the parties (workers in artistic professions, heads of companies, their deputies, and chief accountants, workers classified as dual job holders (*sovmestiteli*), workers elected according to competitive procedures for a particular position, and pensioners). LC RF does not contemplate in the Article 59 the possibility to conclude fixed-term contracts with foreign sportsmen and coaches which might be useful considering that Russian immigration legislation limits the term of work permit for foreign citizens (*see* §9 *infra*). However in practice in case of professional sportsmen there are no particular restrictions and fixed-term contracts can be concluded without taking account of the nature of the work and its performance.

194. If there is no specific agreement on a fixed term, the contacts will be deemed to be open-ended. As for coaches, fixed-term contracts may be concluded only in case of training and the management of competitions aimed at achieving certain results in professional sport or in the hiring of coaches for the national team.[131] There is no minimum term. In addition to Article 57 LC RF on the general terms for the conclusion of employment contracts, Article 348(2) lays down additional requisites to be included in employment contracts with professional sportsmen and women. In particular, employers are required:

- to provide training for sportsmen and women and promote their participation in competitions under the guidance of coaches;
- to make sure that sportsmen and women comply with sports regimes and prepare for competitions;
- to ensure that sportsmen and women take part in competitions only at the employer's request;
- to ensure that sportsmen and women do not to use doping or prohibited substances and that they undergo doping tests;

131. Thus it might be difficult to conclude contracts with coaches in amateur sport.

- to require employers to provide information about their location for doping testing;
- to take out life assurance and medical insurance for their players. They are also required to take out supplementary medical insurance providing sportsmen with medical cover that is additional to the cover provided by compulsory insurance schemes.

195. There is also an obligatory clause to include in contracts with professional coaches concerning the duty to take all the necessary measures to prevent players from violating anti-doping rules.

196. Additional provisions may be included concerning:

- the consent of the sportsmen or women and coaches for their personal data to be kept on file, and a copy of the employment contract to be sent to the All-Russian Sport Federation for the sport in question; in the case of sportsmen/coaches taking part in the national team of the RF, to transmit a copy of the contract to the federal executive body responsible for state policy in the field of sport;
- the requirement to wear outfits provided by the employer while taking part in training and sporting events;
- the requirement to comply with sports competition regulations in relation to employment;
- the requirement of sportsmen to give notice to the employer about the termination of the employment contract at their initiative subject to the terms laid down in Article 348.12 LC RF;
- the amount and nature of any indemnity to be paid to the employer by sportsmen or women in the case of termination of the employment contract pursuant to Article 348.12 LC RF.

197. Moreover, employers are obliged at the time of hiring and for the duration of the employment contract to inform the sportsmen and women about the norms adopted by the All-Russian sports federations, the regulations on sporting competitions, the contractual terms between the employer and sponsors, and the organization of sports meetings, to the extent that they concern the sportsmen and women in their employment. The Regulations on the Status and Transfer of Players also govern employment matters concerning professional football players.

§3. Employment Relationship in Football

198. Contractual terms of the parties according to the Regulations on the Status and Transfer of Players

I. Obligations of Clubs

199. Clubs are under an obligation:

- to pay monthly salaries in full and in a timely manner, and make other payments according to the employment contract and local normative acts regulating bonus payments;
- to provide players with appropriate working conditions according to the labour legislation of RF, collective agreements and individual employment contracts, and FIFA, UEFA and FUR Regulations;
- to ensure players take part in training and competitions under the guidance of a coach;
- to provide the compulsory social insurance for players according to the labour legislation or other normative acts of the RF;
- to cover the cost of health and safety insurance as well as medical insurance in order to enable players to receive medical services in addition to those required by law and to specify their terms;
- to organize at their own expense obligatory preliminary and annual periodical medical check-ups for the player, extra medical check-ups at the request of players and medical advice;
- to ensure training and the participation of players in competitions under the guidance of a coach;
- to provide players with the necessary sports gear and other technical equipment necessary for their activity and to carry out any necessary maintenance;
- to provide financial assistance in the case of a temporary inability to work due to sports-related injury under the employment contract, in order to bring the temporary disability benefit in line with the average monthly salary of players in cases in which this benefit is lower and no income support is provided by supplementary insurance schemes.

Moreover, the amended version of the Regulations on the Status and Transfer of Players (effective from 1 January 2016) introduced into Article 7 a new clause 7^1 laying down for football clubs an obligation in cases in which a player suffers a sports-related injury during a sports event in the course of the validity of the employment contract. In such cases the club is required to cover the following expenses not covered by medical insurance and obligatory medical insurance, with the consent of the club's medical officer (unless otherwise agreed by the parties in the contract):

- expenses in relation to the medical treatment of the player on the RF territory and abroad (if stipulated in the contract), including related travel expenses;
- expenses in relation to the purchase of necessary medical products and individual care;
- expenses covering special external medical care.

II. Obligations of Players

200. Players are under an obligation:

- to comply with the sports programme defined by the club and take part in training for competitions;
- to take part in competitions only as indicated by the football clubs to which they belong;
- to take part in training or other events (including commercial events, meetings and press conferences);
- to travel with the team within the RF and abroad, following the itinerary and using transport provided by the employer;
- to use the equipment made available by the employer for use during working hours;
- to comply with FIFA, UEFA and FUR Regulations on working conditions;
- to comply with internal working rules or local regulations of the employer on working activity;
- to abstain from the use of doping, and to consent to doping tests;
- to abstain from any dangerous kind of sport or other activity without the written authorization of the employer;
- to uphold the reputation of the employer during public meetings and contact with the press;
- to behave in compliance with moral norms in their personal and public life;
- to maintain confidentiality with regard to confidential commercial or other information, including information relating to the terms of employment and transfer contracts, internal documents of the employer or sponsorship contracts;
- to abstain from gambling or any kind of match-fixing;
- to take part in medical check-ups and follow medical advice;
- to give their consent for the transmission of their personal data, including a copy of the employment contract, to the RF or other football league; in case of the appointment of the player to the national team of the RF, to transmit the employment contract to the federal body responsible for state policy in the field of sport.

§4. Remuneration, Working Time and Other Employment Aspects

201. Sportsmen like other employees are subject to the norms of the LC RF as mentioned above, with some specific norms and exceptions. The sportsmen usually have unregulated working hours,[132] but they have a right to a total of twenty-eight days' holiday. Moreover, they have the right to at least four additional calendar days in the case of sportsmen, women and coaches[133] and three calendar days for the unregulated working regime independent of the number of worked hours.[134]

202. Sectoral collective agreement concluded between the Minsport and Profsporttur for 2015–2017 states that coaches whose work positions are included in the professional standard 'Coach'[135] are entitled to no less than fourteen days of

132. Article 101 of the Labour Code of the RF.
133. Article 348.10 of the Labour Code of the RF.
134. Article 119 of the Labour Code of the RF.
135. Approved by the provision of the Ministry of Labour from 07 Apr. 2014 N 193н, except pedagogical coaches (coach – pedagogue, senior coach – pedagogue).

additional paid leave granted in the end of the season which, upon the employee request, can be substituted by the monetary compensation. Longer holidays may be agreed in collective agreements or in individual employment contracts. If the parties so agree, annual holidays may be split in two parts and at least one part should not be shorter than fourteen days. It is possible to recall the worker back from holidays only upon his consent and the part of the non-used vacations should be granted to the worker during a year at the most convenient for him time or in alternative added to the next year holidays. It is prohibited to recall from holidays workers below the age of 18 years, pregnant women and workers employed at works with dangerous or harmful employment conditions. Depending on the professional position, working time may include training activity, individual work with the sportsmen, scientific, creative and research work or other kinds of work foreseen in the work duties or individual plans. It is prohibited to refuse to grant annual paid leave for more than two consecutive years in the case of players below the age of 18.

The same rule is applied to the workers employed at works with harmful conditions. In case of dismissal the employee is entitled to the remuneration for all non-used holidays. Non-used holidays may be granted to the worker at his written request before the dismissal (except the dismissal for the guilty actions).

203. With regard to pay, players receive a fixed monthly salary plus bonuses based on their sporting achievements, in addition to other incentives (e.g., compensations for the transfer in another locality). Often bonuses significantly exceed the basic wage which can be established on quite a low basis. The practice of RFU Chamber in this regards starts to consolidate and corresponds to FIFA parameters. In the decision from 3 June 2010[136] the FUR Chamber supported the claims of the players A, B, C who claimed the omission of paying bonuses for the season 2009 in relation to Russian Championship. These bonuses were paid to all the members of the team in the beginning of 2010 except the claimants who had left the team by this time. The club sustained that the bonuses were not part of the wage and should be left to the employer's discretion. Moreover it claimed that the players were not anymore the part of the team. However the FUR Chamber considered this decision discriminatory since all the other players were remunerated and the claimants were not accused of any disciplinary provisions and obliged the club to pay the bonuses.

204. Sometimes wage terms are fixed not in employment contract but in the annexes which considering norms of sport federations, leagues, federations may be not registered in these bodies. Wage may be also regulated in collective agreements. For example federal sectoral collective agreement for 2012–2014 adopted by Minsport and Profsprottrour on 21 December 2011 establishes wage guarantees for the sportsmen according to Article 348.10 LC RF. In particular Article 6(6) of this agreement states that non-inclusion of the sportsmen into the sport competition (even in cases when sportsman does not correspond to the competition requirements) is a not a reason to reduce his wage. Moreover Article 4(3) of the Agreement states that average wage should be at least four times the minimum subsistence level.

205. The provision of the Ministry of Sport, Tourism and Youth Policy (nowadays Minsport) from 19 July 2010 N. 7491 defines the modality of wage settlement for the

136. It was supported by CAS, *see* CAS2010/A/2204, *Joint stock company Football Club Ural v. Football Union of Russia* in Prokopets et al, *supra* n. 121, 2012, 107.

sportsmen, coaches and other specialists of national teams who are employed in federal budgetary institutions within the jurisdiction of the Ministry of Sport. Under its provisions, sportsmen national team members may have personal additional raising coefficient which is summed to the salary in case of the achievement of certain sport results, complexity of tasks and other factors. The recommended maximum for this coefficient is no more than twenty-five. This coefficient is established only for a determined period during a year and does not affect basic salary or other compensatory payments or other bonuses. Moreover collective agreements may contemplate some payments of compensatory character or stimulating payments. For example sectoral collective agreement concluded by Minsport and Profsporttur for 2015–2017 (*see* Part VI collective bargaining in sport, *infra*) in the Article 5.19 recommends to include following compensatory and stimulatory payments:

- for good results shown by the sportsman during the preparation in sport disciplines included in the programme of Olympic games, Paralympics, Deaflympics or other important sport competitions;
- payments to the young sportsmen up to 50% to the wage and their mentors (coaches) (up to 15% to the wage);
- payments for high work intensity and high results;
- payments for quality of the work done (respect to the efficiency criteria of the organization):

  (a) for the timeliness and completeness of the work duties;
  (b) for the conformity of the work quality to the qualification category and work duties;
  (c) for the personal participation in the activities organized by the organization;
  (d) for the positive feedbacks about the work;
  (e) for organization of more than ten official sport and physical culture events, etc.

- payments for seniority:

  (a) for seniority 5–10 years – from 3% to 5% to the wage;
  (b) for seniority 10–20 years – from 5% to 10% to the wage;
  (c) for seniority 20–25 years – from 10% to 20% to the wage;
  (d) for seniority more than twenty-five years – from 20% to 25% to the wage.

- payments for qualification and experience officially recognized and marked by the state awards:

  (a) for the honorary title 'Honoured worker of physical culture and sport of the RF', for state awards of the Russian Federation and USSR, for the honorary title 'Honoured coach of the RF', 'Honoured master of sports of the RF' and 'Honoured master of sports of the USSR' – from 50% up to 100% to the wage;

(b) for the honorary badge of honour 'For the merits in development of physical culture and sport' – from 40% up to 50%;
(c) for the sport titles 'Master of sports of the RF of international class', 'Master of sports of the USSR of international class', 'Grandmaster of the RF', 'Grandmaster of the USSR', 'Excellent pupil of physical culture and sport' – from 20% up to 40%;
(d) for the scientific degree (like a doctor) and other departmental awards and titles from 10% up to 20%.

206. A number of articles of the Labour Code,[137] Administrative Code,[138] Penal Code[139] as well as those of single sport federations establish responsibility of the employer for non-payment or delay in payment of salaries. In some kinds of sport it can also bring to the application of sport sanctions. In case of football, if the football club does not fulfill his financial duties in relation to a player or other professional football clubs for more than thirty calendar days, the Regulations on the Status and Transfer of Players (Article 8.1.) and Annex 3(Article 9^1) contemplate the following sanctions:

- fine up to RUB 250,000;
- prohibition to register new players whose international transfer certificate is at the FUR, for one registration period;
- prohibition to register new players whose international transfer certificate is at the international football federation, for one registration period.

207. Moreover such violations represent serious infringement of the employment contract by the employer and under the regulations may constitute a justified reason to terminate unilaterally employment relationship on the player's initiative.[140]

208. There are also additional provisions in relation to the Labour Code limitations for professional sportsmen. For example, they concern the practice of *sovmestitelstvo*[141] or working for several employers. According to Article 348.7 LC RF professional sportsmen or coaches need permission from the main employer for this. In case of a temporary transfer of the sportsman to another employer (Article 348.4 LC RF), permission from all employers is required.[142] This limitation concerns only *sovmestitelstvo* on the part of sportsmen/coaches. In theory they may have another job for other activities not related to sport. Persons under 18 years of age are not permitted to work on the basis of such a contract.

137. Article 236, 142 LC RF.
138. Article 5.27 AC RF.
139. Article 145.1. PC RF.
140. Alekseyev, 2014. *supra* n. 17.
141. Article 282 of the LC RF defines it as the performance by the worker of regular work (different from the main job) on the basis of the employment contract during the worker's free time.
142. In the case of other categories of workers, the general rules under Art. 282 LC RF do not require the permission of the employer and do not limit the number of potential employers.

§5. The Termination of the Employment Relationship

209. The termination of employment contracts is one of the most important and controversial matters in professional sport as it may entail serious financial losses for both parties. On the one hand, clubs usually spend a considerable amount on transfer fees to be paid to the player's previous club. On the other hand, players can face difficulties in finding a new club willing to pay substantial transfer fees to the old club. Until recently no special rules on the termination of employment contracts were laid down in the LC RF and Federal Laws, and as a result the general rules on the termination of employment contracts were applied (Article 77 83 LC RF). However, the LC RF leaves the list of possible reasons for termination open.

210. The general rules for the termination of employment contracts at the employee's initiative are laid down in Article 80 LC RF, pursuant to which the employee can inform the employer in writing of his intention to terminate the employment contract two weeks before the expiry date if no other term is laid down by the LC RF or other Federal Law in the case of:

- impossibility to continue employment because of acceptance at an educational institution, or retirement;
- violation by the employer of the labour law norms and other legal provisions containing labour law provisions, local normative measures and terms of the collective agreement or individual employment contract.

211. In the case of professional sportsmen one month's notice is required rather than two weeks as in the case of other workers. In the case of contracts concluded for a period of less than four months, a general two-week period of notice is applicable (Article 348.12 LC RF). However, the regulations of the sport federations may lay down shorter or longer periods of notice.

212. Under the Article 8 of the Regulations on the Status and Transfer of Players, the employment contract between the player and the club can be terminated without penalty or indemnity after the natural termination of the employment contract, or by the agreement between the parties or because of the circumstances beyond their will as well as in other cases specified in the Regulations on the Status and Transfer of Players. In the case of unilateral termination before the expiry of the contract, the party responsible for the breach is required to compensate the other party.

I. Termination with Just Cause

213. The LC RF does not specify what a just cause is, and hence Article 80 LC can be applied by analogy.

214. Considering the specific nature of sport, certain sport-related reasons can justify unilateral termination such as:[143]

143. U. V. Zaitzev, Peculiarities of termination of labour contract with sportsmen, Materials of the *II* International Conference on 'Sports law: perspectives of development', D. I. Rogachev, M. A. Prokopets eds, M, 2009, 65 (In Russian).

- failure to take regular part in competitions, meaning less than 10% of official matches in the season in the case of football;
- failure to include the player in the current season if not related to full or partial inability to play;
- violation by the employer of laws and other normative acts, collective agreements, or the individual employment contract;
- relegation of the club to a lower division;
- exclusion of the club from sporting events;
- reinstatement of the player's amateur status;
- termination of the player's career.

215. These matters were previously governed by the Football Union of Russia regulations in accordance with the relevant FIFA Regulations. Currently, Article 12 of the FUR regulations make more specific provisions for the termination of employment contracts for sport-related reasons. Prior to the recent changes it was possible to terminate the contract of an established football player who played less than 10% of the matches in a given season. Now the contract can be terminated for sport-related reasons by a player who has reached the age of 21. Goalkeepers playing in the season are excluded. Sport-related reasons cannot be applied in cases in which the player played in fewer than 10% of the matches due to:

- temporary inability because of sports injury or health reasons in general;
- sports disqualification and a ban on playing football for a period of more than three months;
- temporary transfer to another club.

216. The position of FIFA in this regard is similar. The only difference of approach is that FIFA calculates 10% of matches in the season considering the number of minutes spent on the field, whereas the Football Union of Russia calculates the number of matches.

217. The termination of the employment contract for sport-related reasons is quite a rare practice. Among the emblematic cases one of *Temile v. Football Club Kriylia Sovetov* (Samara)[144] can be examined. In this case CAS partially uphold the decisions of FIFA DRC concerning the compensation due by the player to the club. Important is that CAS supported the calculation of 10% of the effectively passed on the field-playing time and also introduced a fourth criteria for evaluation of the justifiability of invocation of a sport-related reasons. This fourth criteria is personal player's circumstances. Another important issue is when invocating sport-related reason the player should have demonstrated previously to the club his discontent of not being fielded or fielded not with the main team. The omission (as it was in case of Temile) of this can be regarded as a tacit consent of a player and may significantly undermine the successful outcome of his claim. Another important condition concerns the terms of notification of the player's intention to invoke a sport-related reason (no later than fifteen days after the last official match for which the player was registered).

144. DRC 10 Aug. 2007; CAS 2007/A/1369, Omonigho Temile *v.* FS Kriylia Sovetov Samara, Prokopets et al., *supra* n. 121, 153–160.

218. The regulations also lay down justified reasons for the unilateral termination of the contract by a football player. Previously this was regulated by the Chamber of FUR in specific cases. At present Article 11 of the regulations reflects the case law of the Chamber with regard to justified reasons:

- violation by the club of laws and other normative acts, collective agreements, or the individual employment contract;
- loss of professional status of the club;
- reinstatement of the player's amateur status pursuant to the regulations;
- arrears in the payment of salary of a football player which amount corresponds to two-months' salary or forfeit payment which amount corresponds to two months or more of the player's salary for more than thirty days;
- failure to include a professional player who has turned 18 in the current season not linked to a temporary inability to work, disqualification, or temporary transfer to another club;
- violation of the rights of the player, such as discrimination in relation to other players on the team, including training without the ball or outside the team (not related to the status of the health of the player) and extended exclusion from training activities;
- other violations by the club recognized as violations by the Chamber.

219. The FIFA Regulations do not include a list of justified reasons for termination and each case is considered separately by the FIFA Dispute Resolution Chamber. This approach is reasonable as FIFA has extensive case law that has been consolidated over time.[145]

II. Termination Without Just Cause

220. If a player intends to unilaterally terminate the contract without just reasons, he must pay the employer the corresponding indemnity in cases in which such a clause has been included in the contract. If a time limit for the payment is not agreed upon, it can be settled by the Dispute Resolution Chamber which considers such criteria as (Article 10 of the Regulations on the Status and Transfer of Players):

- salary or other payments due to the player under the employment contract with the current and the new club;
- the remaining period of the contract with the current club;
- expenses of the current club relating to the player;
- whether the termination occurred during the protected period or not;
- other objective criteria.

221. In case of the termination of the employment contract during the protected period without just cause, sports sanctions may be applied.

145. Prokopets et al., *ibid.*

A player intending to terminate the employment contract outside the protected period is required to inform the club within fifteen calendar days of the last official match of the season. (Article 10(5) of the Regulations on the Status and Transfer of Players). Failure to comply with this notice period results in the imposition of sports sanctions in proportion to the length of the period.

222. In case of unilateral termination without just cause by the club, the player has the right to compensation. If the amount has not been previously agreed by the parties, it is determined by the Dispute Resolution Chamber after consideration of the applicable criteria (Article 9 of the Regulations on the Status and Transfer of Players):

- salary or other payments due to the player under the employment contract with the current and future club;
- the remaining period of the contract with the current club;
- expenses of the players relating to the transfer to the new club;
- whether the termination occurred during the protected period or not;
- other objective criteria.

223. The compensation cannot be less than three months' salary unless the remaining period of the employment contract is less than three months (Article 9 of the Regulations on the Status and Transfer of Players). In case of the unilateral termination of the contract by the club without just cause during the protected period, sports sanctions are applied to the club.

224. The individual employment contract can include other clauses: Article 348-12 LC RF establishes that the parties can stipulate in the contract an obligation on the part of a sportsman to compensate the employer in case the contract is terminated at the initiative of the player without justified reason, or at the initiative of the employer in the case of disciplinary sanctions, (Article 192(3) LC RF). In case of disciplinary sanctions the player is also required to compensate the employer.[146] The employer can dismiss the player as a disciplinary sanction for the non-performance or inadequate performance of his contractual duties. Pursuant to Article 348.12 the amount of this compensation can be determined as two months' salary if the contract does not provide otherwise.

225. However, there are frequent abuses by clubs in the case of the dismissals and they often make use of the pretext of disciplinary sanctions,[147] as in the cases of David Mujiti and Igor Strelkov. These cases demonstrate the power of clubs to dismiss players unilaterally without justified reason. As a result, stronger legal regulation of this matter appears to be needed.

---

146. Paragraphs 5, 6, 9 or 10 Art. 81 LC RF, comma 1 Art. 336 LC RF, 7, 8 Art. 81 if the actions were committed at the workplace in course of employment.

147. *See* the cases of: David Mujiri (Contractual dispute petition of D. Mujiri, 02 Feb. 2010) and Igor Strelkov (Statement of professional player Igor Strelkov d/d 29 Apr. 2011), O. Rymkevich and N. Grammatikov, *The Regulation of Employment Contracts for Professional Football Players: The Case of Russia*, in European Sports Law and Policy Bulletin, I-2011.

§6. Disciplinary Rules and Sanctions

226. Following the introduction of the new section in the LC RF, pursuant to Article 348.11 LC RF there are additional clauses permitting termination of the contract with players, known as sports reasons:

- disqualification of six months or more;
- use (even just a single instance) of doping ascertained in the course of doping tests according to the federal laws;

227. These reasons for dismissal are classified as disciplinary sanctions and as a result a specific procedure pursuant to Article 193 LC RF must be implemented.

Disqualification under the Federal Law on Physical Culture and Sport of the RF[148] results in the exclusion of sportsmen from competitions by the All-Russian Sport Federation. This may occur because of the violation of the rules for some sports or norms adopted by international and national sport federations. This decision may be adopted by Russian Federations for various kinds of sport, including the Football Union of Russia. In this regard the Disciplinary Regulations of FUR (2010)[149] (Article 17) can be mentioned. The disqualification for a match (prohibition for participation in the match or competition) can be applied for a number of matches, days, months or years. In the absence of other provisions, normally it cannot exceed twenty-four matches or two years. If it is combined with a fine, disqualification will be prolonged until the fine is not paid out in a full amount.

228. In the case of a disqualification for a period of less than six months the contract cannot be terminated. There is no maximum limit for disqualification as it is possible to impose a lifetime disqualification (for a second case of doping), in accordance with the International Anti-Doping Code (Copenhagen, 2003)[150] obligatory for sportsmen and women all over the world.

The following sanctions[151] are provided in section 3 of the Disciplinary Regulations of the Football Union of Russia:

I. Natural and Legal Persons

229.

(a) reprimand;
(b) fine;
(c) withdrawal of titles and awards.

148. 4 Dec. 2007 329-FS.
149. With the latest amendments from 22 Jun. 2016, N. 159/6 effective from 3 Mar. 2017.
150. www.wada.ama.org, new reduction from 1 Jan. 2009.
151. The offences and sanctions are listed in appendix No. 3 to the Regulations on the Status and Transfer of Players.

II. Natural Persons

230.

- reprimand;
- expulsion from a competition;
- disqualification;
- prohibition of any football-related activity;
- prohibition of access to the stadium.

III. Legal Persons

231.

- obligation to play a match (or matches) behind closed doors;
- obligation to play a match (or matches) in a neutral venue;
- annulment of a match result;
- assignment of a defeat;
- deduction of points;
- expulsion from competitions;
- relegation to a lower division.

232. Annex 3 of the Regulation on the Status and Transfer of Players provides a list of offences and corresponding sanctions (our translation):

No.	*Offences under the FUR Regulation on the Status and Transfer of Players*	*Sanction*
1	Conclusion by the player of two or more professional employment contracts for the same period (excluding the 'leasing' of players to another club)	Disqualification for four to six months
2	Conclusion by the player of an employment contract with the club to which they were transferred for any period exceeding the leasing contract	Ban on the registration of new players for the new football club for a maximum of two registration periods
3	Conclusion by the player and club to which they were transferred on the basis of a leasing contract of the actions aimed to transfer the player to a third club	Fine for the new club of up to RUB 500,000

No.	*Offences under the FUR Regulation on the Status and Transfer of Players*	*Sanction*
4	Termination of the employment contract before the established term at the players' initiative during the protected period, or shortcomings on the part of the player during the protected period resulting in the termination of the contract by the club	
5	Failure of the player to comply with the term of notice of the club or contractual termination before the established term due to sport reasons or reinstatement of the player's amateur status	Disqualification of the player for a period from one to three months
6	Failure on the part of the club to comply with the terms of the transfer contract or transfer leasing contract including transfer fees	Fine for the club of up to RUB 250,000
7	Termination before the permitted term of the employment contract during the protected period and non-payment by the club of the salary or the coach for a period exceeding two months	Ban on the registration of new players for a club for a maximum of two registration periods
8	Violation by the club of the terms of training compensation payment or non-payment	Deduction of points from the club
9	Violation by the club of the terms of solidarity fee payment or non-payment	
9[1]	Violation by the football club of his financial obligations in relation to the play or another club for more than thirty days	–fine up to RUB 250,000 –prohibition to register new players whose international transfer certificate is at the FUR, for one registration period –prohibition to register new players whose international transfer certificate is at the international football federation, for one registration period
10	Violation by the player of the terms of compensation fee for the termination of contract before the permitted term	Fine of up to RUB 250,000

No.	*Offences under the FUR Regulation on the Status and Transfer of Players*	*Sanction*
11	Failure of the club to comply with the terms of registration laid down in the employment contract with the player	Fine of up to RUB 100,000
12	Failure to execute or failure to execute in a timely manner the decisions of the FUR Committee on the Status of Players or of the Dispute Resolution Chamber	Fine of up to RUB 300,000 Deduction of points Disqualification of the player for a period from four to six months
13	Failure to provide the player with a copy of the employment contract on the day of stipulation	Fine for the club up to RUB 100,000
14	Failure to provide the player with a copy of the employment contract with all amendments or annexes	Fine for the club up to RUB 100,000
15	Violation of the rules on the transfer of players (Article 17 of the Regulations)	Disqualification of the player for a period from four to six months
		Ban on the registration of new players with the new club for a maximum of two registration periods Fine for the new club of up to RUB 500,000
16	Failure to comply with the rules on extrajudicial regulation of disputes relating to the Regulations on the Status and Transfer of Players	Ban on the registration of new players for a club for a maximum of two registration periods Disqualification of the player or coach for a period from three to six months
17	Failure on the part of the club to comply with the duty to send players to the national team of the RF	Fine for the club of up to RUB 500,000 Assignment of a defeat on the club for all the matches in which the player took part (annulment of all points gained in such matches or award of victory to the opposing club in case of cup games)
18	Violation by the player of the terms of temporary transfer from the football club to the national team	Fine for a player of up to RUB 250,000

No.	*Offences under the FUR Regulation on the Status and Transfer of Players*	*Sanction*
19	Failure to comply with the registration procedures by an official of the organization required to register players	Fine for such officials from RUB 1,000 to RUB 15,000

233. The application of the sanctions for disciplinary offences is carried out by the FUR Disciplinary Committee and the FUR Appeal Committee.[152] The Disciplinary Committee of the FUR acts as a Court of First Instance in the case of disciplinary offences and also deals with claims concerning decisions of the jurisdictional bodies of the federations. The Appeals Committee deals with claims concerning the decisions of the Disciplinary Committee of the FUR. An appeal against decisions by the Disciplinary Committee can be made to the Appeals Committee except when they are deemed to be final under the regulations or other norms of the FUR. Decisions of these bodies can be contested at the CAS in Lausanne, and the decisions of this court must be recognized by the parties involved. The CAS or other arbitration courts whose competence is recognized by the FUR Executive Committee act as courts of last instance with regard to the decisions of the Appeals Committee of FUR, decisions of jurisdictional bodies of the interregional confederations of regional football federations or the Disciplinary Committee.

Article 29 of the Regulations on the Status and Transfer of Players (2016) lays down the possibility for the FUR Chamber or Committee to submit, via the FUR, in accordance with the FIFA Regulations on the Status and Transfer of Players, a request to impose sports sanctions on a football club, player or coach anywhere in the world.

234. The CAS or other arbitration court recognized by the Executive Committee cannot deal with the following matters:[153]

- claims relating to the violation of the rules of the game;
- sanctions of less than five matches or three months;
- cases under consideration are already under examination in another court of arbitration recognized by the FUR on the RF territory.

§7. Medical Issues

235. Article 348.3 LC RF regulates medical check-ups for sportsmen and women. Before the conclusion of the employment contract sportsmen are subject to an obligatory medical examination. During their employment relationship they are subject to periodical medical check-ups in order to ascertain and prevent occupational diseases.

236. Employers are under the obligation to organize at their own expense obligatory preliminary and annual periodical medical examinations of the player, extra medical check-ups at the request of players and medical advice. Players continue to receive their salary during absences relating to medical check-ups. Sportsmen are

152. The jurisdictional bodies in football (s. III, Ch. 6 of the Disciplinary Regulations of FUR).
153. Article 40(2) of the Disciplinary Regulations of FUR.

obliged to attend these check-ups and follow medical advice. Analogous provisions are contained in the Regulations on the Status and Transfer of Players (Article 7(12) for the players and Article 7(11) for the clubs).

237. The refusal by sportsmen to undergo these check-ups is deemed to be a breach of discipline with corresponding sanctions, while repeated avoidance without justified reasons may result in legitimate dismissal. According to Article 76 LC RF the employer is required to exempt from work an employee who has not passed an obligatory check-up. In cases in which failure to pass a medical check-up may be imputed to a fault on the part of the player, the player is not paid for the entire period up to the check-up. If players fail to pass a check-up for reasons not depending on their own actions, they are paid two-thirds of normal salary as in case of obligatory exemption from work.

238. It is prohibited to terminate employment contract with the sportsman who temporary lost his ability to work for health reasons.

The decision of the FUR Chamber of 11 February 2011 when club insisted on terminating the contract with a football player because prior to signing the contract the player had concealed information about a previous injury was held to be illegitimate.

In the opinion of the Chamber, the club had sufficient opportunities to carry out all necessary check-ups before the stipulation of the contract and by its signing it consequently assumed all the associated risks. Moreover before the consequences of this injury became known the player had already successfully played for the team seven matches.[154]

239. Generally FIFA has a clear position regarding this issue which is expressed in the Article 18(4) of the regulations stating: 'The validity of a contract may not be made subject to a successful medical examination and/or the grant of a work permit,' thus it establishes additional sportsmen guarantees. The employer has to carry out all necessary check-ups before the stipulation of the contract. The practice of FUR Chamber on dispute resolution conforms to FIFA position.[155]

§8. Transfer of Players

240. At present, certain controversial matters such as the transfer of players are not regulated by law.[156] Even the appropriate terms are absent from the legal provisions. Neither definition of the legal nature of the transfer contract is provided in the 'Law on Sport' in the RF, nor in the special section of the Labour Code, and it remains doubtful whether it should be regulated by norms of commercial or labour law. In the Labour Code only temporary transfers to another employer are mentioned (Article 348.4 LC RF).

154. Prokopets et al. *supra* n. 121, 2012, 83.
155. Prokopets et al., *supra* n. 121, 84.
156. U. V. Zaitzev, *Legal Nature of the Transfer of Sportsmen: Sport, economics, law and management*, 2009 (in Russian). (Ю. В. Зайце, в *Правовая природа переходов спортсмена* // Спорт, экономика, право, управление, 2009).

I. Temporary Transfer of Players to Another Employer (Article 348.4 LC RF)

241. In cases where the employer cannot ensure the participation of players in competitions, it is possible to transfer them on a temporary basis to another employer for a period of no more than one year. Among other conditions the written consent of the sportsman for temporary transfer and agreement with the future club is required. Article 348.4 covers only sportsmen and not coaches. The introduction of this special clause in the Labour Code is important as Russian labour legislation allows only a direct employment relationship between employer and employee. Even temporary agency work has been prohibited till recently and the adopted law bringing it under strict control will become effective only on 1 January 2016.[157]

During this period, the temporary employer concludes a fixed-term contract (pursuant to Article 348.2 LC RF) with the player, while the contract with the main employer is suspended and consequently all the rights and obligations ensuing from the employment contract and collective agreement are suspended, with the exception of the matters regulated by Article 348.7[158] of the LC RF. The terms of the original employment contract continue to apply. After the expiry of the temporary transfer, the original employment contract enters into force again, from the date immediately after the termination of the temporary transfer. In the course of the transfer, both the player and the employer are required to comply with the rules laid down by labour law and other normative acts. The temporary employer cannot transfer the player to a third party. In the case of premature termination of the fixed-term contract, the original contract comes back into force the next day. If upon termination the player continues to work for the employer to whom he/she had been temporarily transferred and none of the parties requests termination of the relationship, the original contract is terminated and the temporary contract is prolonged for a period agreed by the parties. In the absence of an agreement on a fixed term, the temporary transfer contract is deemed to be concluded for an indefinite period. The employer may also refuse to renew the contract upon termination, but it is not clear how players can safeguard their rights. LC RF does not provide special norms of responsibility in the case of violation of the rules of temporary transfer (e.g., if the player does not return to the previous employer) nor specific sanctions in this regard which in practice deprives all the parties of this triangular relationship of the necessary guarantees. It is especially relevant point in case of international transfers since LC RF does not have extraterritorial validity.

157. Federal Law 116-FZ from 22 Apr. 2014 'On amending separate legislative acts of the Russian Federation' which will enter into force on 1 Jan. 2016.

158. Article 348.7 LC RF, Peculiarities of combining jobs with other employers of sportsmen and coaches *(sovmestitelstvo)*. Sportsmen and coaches have a right to take up employment as sportsmen and coaches with other employers only with the permission of the main employer. During the temporary transfer, permission must be obtained both from the main employer and temporary one.

II. Temporary Transfer of Player on the Basis of the Contract of 'Leasing' According to the Regulations on the Status and Transfer of Players (2011)

242. A similar scheme is contemplated in the regulations (Article 19). The transfer of a football player on the basis of the contract of leasing is provided in Article 1 of the regulations which defines it as transfer of football player from professional football club with which he is registered in another professional football club for temporary performance in favour of the latter. Article 19(2) states that in case of leasing the player and the club for which he is registered can choose either:

- to suspend the existing employment contract with the club and stipulate an agreement on temporary transfer to another club under LC RF (Article 348.4, *see* paragraph 241 *supra*); or
- to terminate before expiry the existing employment contract and stipulate a new one with the deferred date of the beginning (after the termination of the player's performance for another club).

The transfer contract in the form of leasing may include:

- transfer fees to be paid by the professional football club to which the player is temporarily leased in favour of the club with which he is registered;
- full or partial compensation paid by the club to which the player was leased;
- other provisions not in contrast with the legislation of the RF, FIFA Regulations and FUR Regulations.

The minimum term of temporary performance for another club based on leasing is the period between the first and second registration period or the time between the second registration period and the end of the current season.

The obligatory templates for the contracts of leasing are provided in the Annexes 6 and 7 of the regulations. Additional provisions may be included if they are not in contrast with the regulations.

As an additional guarantee for the club with which the player is registered, the regulations (Article 19(5)) prohibit the player and the club to which he was temporary leased from concluding a contract the duration of which exceeds the duration of the contract of leasing. Moreover the club to which the player was leased does not have a right to undertake any action aimed at the player's transfer to another football club, or transfer him to another club without the written authorization of the main club and the player.

Such norms are supported by sanctions which are absent in Article 348.4 LC RF. So in case of violation the player and the club to which he was leased have a joint obligation to pay compensation to the main professional football club calculated as if it were a premature termination of the contract at the player's initiative, unless it is otherwise agreed in the leasing contract. In addition the new club is obliged to pay training compensation. Finally the sanctions can also be applied to both the player and the new club.

Pursuant to Article 19(8) the transfer of the player from one club to another by leasing is considered as one transfer and a return to the previous club is not deemed to be a transfer under these regulations.

III. Transfers of Players According to the Regulations on the Status and Transfer of Players (2011)

243. As mentioned before, in the absence of legislative regulation, the solutions to any problems regarding transfers are to be sought in the regulations of the sports federations containing specific norms regulating the working conditions of professional players that are lacking in federal laws. In particular, transfers of players are regulated by norms of international federations that must be complied with by national federations. In this regard the regulations of the Football Union of Russia (Regulations on the Status and Transfer of Players, 2011)[159] include norms on the transfer of football players. They define transfers as relations regulated by FIFA and the Regulations on the Status of Transfer of Players linked to the change by the player of the football club (or sports academy) the player is registered with. As a result transfers are governed by sports regulations and relate to the registration of the player with the club in order to take part in the competitions.

According to Article 2, the regulations cover the following matters:

- the status of football players registered with clubs (and sports academies) participating in competitions under the aegis of the FUR;
- the registration of football players for clubs (and sports academies) participating in competitions under the aegis of the FUR;
- the transfer of football players from clubs (and sports academies) taking part in competitions under the aegis of the FUR to other clubs (and sports academies) participating in competitions under the aegis of the FUR;
- reimbursement of the cost of training players to the clubs (and sports academies) participating in competitions under the aegis of the FUR;
- dispute resolution among football stakeholders including clubs and sports academies taking part in competitions under the aegis of the FUR, players registered with clubs taking part in competitions under the aegis of the FUR, coaches registered with clubs taking part in competitions under the aegis of the FUR, football agents licensed by the FUR.

IV. Transfer Fees, Training Compensation and Solidarity Mechanism

244. Under Article 18(3) of the regulations, in relation to transfers, a transfer fee can be applied. However clubs may also opt not to apply any fee. The transfer fee should be paid to professional football clubs. The new club has to pay the transfer fee within thirty calendar days (unless otherwise agreed in the transfer contract) after the

159. Available at: http://www.rfs.ru/rfs/documents/strategies (in Russian) (accessed 30 Jul. 2017). Latest amendments 3 Mar. 2017 No. 166/9.

date the transfer contract becomes effective. In case the club does not respect this term the following sanctions can be applied under Annex 3 of the regulations:

- fine of up to RUB 250,000;
- ban on the registration of new players for a club for a maximum of two registration periods;
- deduction of points from the club.

A. *Transfer Fees*

245. Moreover in the case of a delay in payment the new club has to pay to the former club the penalty considering the refinancing rate of the central bank of the RF for the day of the decision, if another sanction is not established in the transfer contract (Article 18(3)). The club is not entitled to transfer the right to the transfer fee to third parties. Under Article 18(7) no club can conclude a contract allowing another part of the contract or third parties to influence its independence in labour or transfer relations or teams sport performance. Disciplinary sanctions can be applied by the FIFA Disciplinary Committee for the violation of this provision.

B. *Training Compensation*

246. Another important kind of fee is compensation for training. This fee pursuant to Article 21(1) of the regulations should be paid to all football clubs (sport academies) in case football player signs his first professional contract or is subject to a transfer to another professional football club before the end of the season when he reaches the age of 23. Only clubs (sport academies) who participated in the education and training of the player and are included in his football player ‘passport’ are entitled to such compensation.

The new edition of the regulations (2011) increased the training compensation to be paid to the football club on signing the first professional contract. Previously, pursuant to the regulations of 2006 when players signed their first contract, the amateur football club or school was entitled to receive RUB 100,000 multiplied by the coefficient of the new football club: a multiple of three for premier league clubs, two for first division clubs, one for second division clubs. As a result, the maximum training compensation was RUB 300,000. This amount was paid only to the last club (sports academy) the player was registered with.

At present, pursuant to Article 22 of the regulations (as amended 2017), the basic training compensation is calculated on the basis of the number of years the player was registered with the club (or sports academy) in the period from 10 to 21 years[160] considering the age of the player as follows:

160. Following the last amendments of the Regulations of 30 Mar. 2015 the age for the calculation of training compensation and solidarity mechanisms was changed from 12 to 10 years. Then it was periodically adjusted (*see* latest version of the Regulations from 3 Mar. 2017 No. 166/9.

Calendar Year of Player's Birthday	*Amount (Rubbles)*
10 years	25,000
11 years	25,000
12 years	25,000
13 years	25,000
14 years	25,000
15 years	25,000
16 years	50,000
17 years	50,000
18 years	50,000
19 years	50,000
20 years	50,000
21 years	50,000

This amount should be multiplied by the club's coefficient (Annex 1 to the regulations). It establishes the following coefficients for clubs where the player is transferred or with which he concludes the contract:

- for clubs of first category: three (professional football clubs of Professional Football League);
- for clubs of second category: two (professional football clubs of the first division of the Federal National League);
- for clubs of third category: one (professional football clubs of the second division or other professional clubs);
- for clubs of fourth category (amateur): no training compensation.

In cases in which the legal person with which the player signs his first contract before the age of 23 has several clubs with a different coefficient, the highest coefficient is applied.

Due to this amendment the final training compensation to be paid to the football clubs that trained the player increased and all the clubs receive compensation, and not just the last club as was previously the case. These provisions are in accordance with FIFA requirements.

According to the new rules no training compensation should be paid after the age of 23 with one exception. Under Article 23 of the regulations, training compensation must be paid to the club the player is leaving only if in the sixty calendar days prior to the expiry of the contract in the season when the player reaches the age of 23, the club offered the player a new contract with terms equivalent to or better than the terms of the expiring contract. In cases in which the player turns down the offer of a new contract, at the time of the transfer the club that the player is leaving receives compensation for training, but the calculation rules have been changed. Now this amount is calculated according to the player's salary and expenses on his medical treatment, without considering any extra remuneration, multiplied by the number of years spent with the club (but no more than five years). The new measure abolished the multiplication on the coefficient of the new club. This is an important innovation in favour of young players, as in the past substantial transfer fees were required. No training compensation is due if the club does not offer a new contract.

The obligatory template for the contract on training compensation is to be found in Annex 8 of the regulations. This compensation must be paid within thirty calendar days of the registration of the player in the professional club unless otherwise agreed in the contract. The violation of this term is subject to the sanctions applied to the club in the case of violation of terms of transfer fees.

Also the terms of claim of this right are limited to twelve months after the player signs his first contract as professional. This money is paid to the FUR which should use it for the development of young football players. The club should use at least 50% from the compensation for training for the coaches who trained the player.

C. Solidarity Mechanism

247. The solidarity mechanism was included in the regulations (2011) and is valid only for transfers within the RF. It is contained in the Chapter 7, Article 24 of the regulations. In case of transfer of professional player to another club (new club) before the expiry of the contract with the previous club (including leasing of the player), all football clubs (sport academies) participating in the competitions of FUR, where this player was trained, except the previous club which the player is intended to leave, have a right to a solidarity fee according to Article 24(3). The new club of the player has to pay 5.5% of the transfer fee or any other compensation due to the previous football club except for training compensation, as a solidarity fee which should be distributed according to Article 24(3) among all the clubs (sport academies) participating in player's training (except the previous club).

If the player transfers to the new club before the expiry of the contract with the previous club (including leasing) and he is below the age of 23 or if a player below the age of 23 was trained in the previous club, the solidarity compensation may be 5.5% of the transfer fee or any other compensation.

The solidarity fee is calculated in addition to the transfer fee or any other compensation specified in the transfer contract unless otherwise agreed.

According to Article 24(3) the following amounts are established depending on the number of years (if less than one year it must be proportionally reduced) in which the player was registered with the football club (sports academy):

Calendar Year of Player's Birthday	*Amount (Rubbles)*
10 years	0.25%
11 years	0.25%
12 years	0.25%

Calendar Year of Player's Birthday	*Amount (Rubbles)*
13 years	0.25%
14years	0.25%
15 years	0.25%
16 years	0.5%
17years	0.5%
18 years	0.5%
19 years	0.5%
20 years	0.5%
21 years	0.5%
22 years	0.5%
23 years	0.5%

The right to the solidarity fee and burden of proof is granted to the interested club (sports academy). In case of its reorganization under the civil law, its successor maintains the right to receive this compensation if all the rights and duties of its predecessor were duly transferred to him. Also the clubs where the player was registered before the age of 23 under the contract of leasing have a right to solidarity compensation. Solidarity compensation is also to be paid in case of mutual exchange of players between clubs.

Also as in case of training compensation, the interested club (sports academy) has twelve months from the moment of the registration of the player with the new club to claim solidarity compensation. In case of violation of this term or in case of impossibility for any reason to compensate the club (academy) participating in the player's training, the new club should pay this fee to the FUR which has to use this money for the support of coaches of young players and improving their qualification.

Unlike training compensation which is not paid if the player stipulates his first contract with professional football club or changes it after the season when he is 23 years old, solidarity compensation should be paid in any case when the player changes club regardless of his age.

V. The Football Player's 'Passport'

248. The passport of the football player (Article 15 of the regulations) is a document certifying the player's membership in the football club which should comply with the laws of RF and requirements of FIFA and FUR. It is managed electronically with the use of the unified electronic system approved by the FUR Executive Committee. The FUR, or any Football League authorized by the FUR running competitions in which the interested sports club participates, are responsible for the registration of professional players and their passports. FUR must give to the club with which the player is registered the passport of the player with all chronological information on clubs (sport academies where he was registered from 10 years old).[161] It is an essential document for determination of the professional affiliation of the player and his carreer achievement as well as for the calculation of training compensation and solidarity fees.

249. More detailed regulations on the football player's passport are provided in the FUR provision N. 151/4 from 28 June 2013 on football players' 'passportization'. The passport should contain the following data:

- surname
- name
- patronymic
- sex
- date of birth
- place of birth
- status of player
- date of the status registration
- unified number of the player
- date of the registration of the unified number
- citizenship
- second citizenship (if any)
- club
- legal details of the club
- type of the club
- category of the club
- fiscal code of the club
- registration number of the club
- city
- federal district
- subject of the federation
- interregional association
- role (type) of the player
- photo
- internal passport and its details (with the electronic scanned copy)
- foreign passport and its details (with the electronic scanned copy)
- record of service (record of service (with the electronic scanned copy)
- annex to the record of service (with the electronic scanned copy)
- birth certificate (with the electronic scanned copy)
- residence address
- passport of parents and its details (with the electronic scanned copy)
- employment contract, type, number, date of start and expiry
  transfer contract type, number, date of start and expiry
- mark on completion of the employment/transfer/leasing contract

161. Following the last amendments of the Regulations of 30 Mar. 2015 the age for the calculation of training compensation and solidarity mechanisms was changed from 12 to 10 years but in the FUR provision N. 151/4 from 28 Jun. 2013 the age of 12 still appears.

250. The passport of the football player is used for:

- player's registration with the football club (sport academy) participating in the competitions under the aegis of FUR;
- player's transfer from one club (academy) to another;
- calculation of solidarity and training compensation.

251. The registration and administration of professional players is carried out by the FUR while the passports of amateurs are managed by the regional football federation (RFF) on the territory where the amateur club (academy) is situated. Each player is assigned an identification number and all the information is kept updated in the 'real time' regime. Both the player and club (academy) are responsible for the reliability of the data provided while FUR and RFF are responsible for the timeliness and correctness of the data inclusion. The services relating to passports are paid and the amounts are established by FUR on a differentiated basis. Professional football players have to pay an annual fee by 1 July each year. Such a payment may be made voluntarily by the club/academy. In case of indebtedness of the player he cannot be allowed to play in competitions.

252. According to Article 15(5) of the regulations the passport should be presented by the FUR, the league concerned or the RFF at the player's registration and within two working days at the player's written request unless otherwise agreed by FUR provisions.

§9. The Status of Foreign Players and Discrimination

253. Since discrimination is a wide-ranging and complex issue, in the present study we will consider it only with regard to international football players in Russia in the context of the norms regulating their work and residence permits, and their employment rights compared to national players.

254. Formally discrimination is prohibited in the Russian Federation by a number of legislative acts. At the international level Russia has ratified ILO core Convention N. 111(1958)[162] and is a party to international agreements with the European Union, Belorussia and Kazakhstan.

Article 19 of the Constitution of the RF prohibits any limitation of the rights of the citizens:

(1) All people shall be equal before the law and court.
(2) The state shall guarantee the equality of rights and freedoms of men and citizens, regardless of sex, race, nationality, language, origin, property and official status, place of residence, religion, convictions, membership of public associations and also of other circumstances. All forms of limitations of human rights on social, racial, national, linguistic or religious grounds shall be banned.

162. Discrimination (Employment and Occupation) Convention, 1958 (No. 111), ratified by Russian Federation on 04 May 1961.

(3) Men and women shall enjoy equal rights and freedoms and have equal possibilities to exercise them.

255. Article 3 of the Labour Code upholds equal opportunities in labour rights for all individuals:

Everyone shall have equal opportunities to implement their labour rights.

Nobody may be subject to restrictions in labour rights and liberties or gain any advantage regardless of sex, race, colour of skin, nationality, language, origin, property, family, social status and occupational position, age, place of residence, attitude to religion, political views, affiliation or failure to affiliate with public associations, as well as other circumstances not pertaining to the business properties of the employee.

Discrimination does not apply in the case of differences, exceptions, preferences, as well as restrictions of the rights of employees determined by specific requirements for the given type of work specified in federal law, or stipulated by the state with respect to persons in need of greater social and legal protection.

Persons who consider that they have been subject to discrimination in the labour sphere may apply to a court to restore the violated rights, reimburse material damage and compensate for the moral damage.

256. The ban of discrimination in sport is stated also in the Article 3(5) of the Law on Sport.

257. Federal Law of 29 June 2015 N. 202 Introducing Article 20.3 and Article 20.4 in the law on Sport establishes the limitations for the players who are not allowed to take part in sports competitions in Russia in international and All-Russia sports competitions for team sports. The law grants the Russian Ministry of Sport the right to establish and coordinate limits on such players competing in Russia separately for each kind of sport in collaboration with the All-Russian Sports Leagues and Federations.

258. The law also lays down obligatory criteria for the general number of players not allowed to represent national Russian teams who can simultaneously take part in competition according to the rules of a given sport. They concern the overall number of sportsmen and women who can be registered with the sports organization for a competition (in accordance with competition regulations) foreign player's athletic qualifications, age, period of permanent stay in Russia, as well as the period of training in Russia and results achieved in competitions for Russian sports organizations. The organizers of sport competitions must include in their regulations the requirement to respect the limitations imposed on the participation of foreign players, apply sanctions in the case of violations and provide information to the Ministry of Sport about the sanctions.

259. Moreover, Article 16(7) of the 'Law on Sport' states that sports federations can adopt restrictions on participation in All-Russian sports competitions for players who do not have right to compete in the national teams of RF according to the norms of international sport organizations taking part in international competitions.

260. Accordingly, Russian football regulations lay down a limit on the employment of international players known as 'legionnaires'. Arguably there is no commonly accepted definition of legionnaire neither in sport nor in the RF nor at the international level. According to the regulation,[163] the term 'legionnaire' indicates an individual who does not have a Russian passport or citizenship of the RF but has a duly registered transfer certificate and employment contract with a club. Legionnaires do not have the right to play for the national teams.

261. Since the 2013–2014 season the FUR has adopted a more restrictive interpretation of 'legionnaires' who will no longer be entitled to represent the Russian national team. This reflects the FIFA norms in this regard. Pursuant to this new interpretation, a 'legionnaire' is defined as a player who has previously played in the national team of another country, even at junior level.[164] Whereas before legionnaires were normally foreign nationals or players with dual citizenship, now even a Russian citizen can lose the right to represent the national team on the basis of this definition.

262. At present it is possible for a football club to have up to six legionnaires on the field (6+5 scheme) that means that not more than six foreign players could be simultaneously playing for one club on the field during the match time.[165] Recently[166] new law was adopted in relation to the regulation of the modality of attraction of foreign sportsmen and coaches and other specialist in winter and summer kinds of sport for work in the Russian Federation (so-called Law on legionnaires). Under this law organizations of physical culture and All-Russian sport federations will be able to attract high-level specialists in sport according to the list of the professional positions of foreign and stateless persons, approved by Minsport. The law itself does not establish limits or quota but regulates rather the process of setting forth of these norms and quota which ideally should be adapted to particular kinds of sport. It also introduces the evaluation scale for the legionnaires which includes qualification, age, period of the stay of the sportsman in Russia and demonstrated sport results. The main ratio of the new law, besides the general aim to improve the procedures of attracting specialists in sport, is to valorize and raise the competitiveness of the national sportsmen.

263. Moreover in this way the FUR imposes the obligation to comply with national labour legislation and regulate the related disputes directly on football clubs. Such an obligation exists also in the Kontinental Hockey League which adopts a

163. Regulation SOGAZ of the Russian Football Championship among the premier league clubs for 2011/2012, S. V. Alekseyev, *supra* n. 17, 2012, 318.
164. Regulations of SOGAZ- Russian Championship of football for Russian premier league for season 2013–2014, regulations of the Russian National Football League adopted by the Decree of FUR 28 Jun. 2013.
165. The first limit on legionnaires in football was introduced in November 2005, with seven international players plus four Russian nationals. In 2009 it was changed to six international players plus five Russian nationals. From 4 Jul. 2012 the FUR returned to the previous scheme (seven + four). So the scheme 7 +4 was effective from 2006 to 2009 and from 2012 to 2015. From July 2015 again 6+5 scheme was adopted. This limit probably will be changed again for the period 2018–2019. The proposed changes will concern the limit on registering players by the clubs rather than a quota of players allowed to play simultaneously in the pith. Different proposals were set forth such as 10+15 and 8+17. However the final decision in this regard is still expected to be taken, http://tass.com/sport/956018. Also in Hockey the actual limit is five foreign players.
166. 19 Jun. 2015 was approved in third reading by the state Duma. It introduces amendments to the 'Law on Sport' and the Law on the Legal Status of Foreign Citizens.

different definition of legionnaires, simply referring to the 'status of foreign player'.[167] This status is assigned to a player who is not entitled to represent Russian national teams, with exceptions for players who satisfy the following criteria:

- at the time of registration the player has a contract in force with KHL signed in 2011/2012 or before;
- at the moment of registration the player has played for not less than two seasons with KHL but not with foreign player status.

264. The question is becoming more problematic as at various levels of competition there are different limits[168] for legionnaires. Considering the rotation among clubs, the employers (clubs) have to dismiss legionnaires in order to comply with the regulations of the competitions at the established level which may result in the violation of labour rights of the players and consequent disputes.[169]

265. The new limitations under which Russian citizens may be deprived of the right to represent national teams can be considered unconstitutional (Articles 37 and 62 of the RF Constitution) especially regarding the rights of Russian citizen, dual citizenship holders or those who refused another citizenship but in the past represented the international teams. As a result also the rights of national sports federations to take decisions in this regard can be contested.

266. Another recent and highly debatable measure concerns taxes for legionnaires and foreign coaches. The tax on foreign coaches was introduced from 1 July 2013 and amounts to RUB 5,000,000 for Russian football premier league coaches and RUB 2,500,000 for National Football League players to be paid by the club to the FUR. As for legionnaires the tax amounts to RUB 500,000 for each player in the premier league. Such a tax is not a new measure as it already existed in hockey. In 2006 hockey clubs paid to the national hockey federation RUB 1,500,000, and for each goalkeeper, RUB 4,500,000. For this reason the clubs left the competitions under the aegis of the national federations and set up the KHL. This problem exists also in basketball. It is called the tax on the players' 'passportization' and it is progressive depending on the number of foreign players: RUB 120,000 for the first legionnaire, 180,000 for the second, 720,000 for the third, 1,440,000 for the fourth, 3,600,000 for the fifth and 5,600,000 for the sixth. The clubs refused to pay the Russian basketball federation and filed an appeal with the courts. The case is still pending.[170]

267. However, the limit on the employment of legionnaires may be struck down by the courts as a discriminatory measure since according to Article 3 LC RF only Federal Law can place limitations on the right to work.[171] Moreover, Article 348(1)

---

167. Article 15 of the legal regulation of KHL.
168. For example in the regulation of Russian Championship of clubs of Professional Football League for 2013-2014 the participation of legionnaires may be completely or partly prohibited.
169. *See* I. Shabanov, *Legionnaires- citizens*, *VII* International Conference 'Globalisation of sport: Olympic games and international competitions', Moscow, 2013.
170. http://www.ftbl.ru/blogs/andrey-vdovin/delo-na-100-millionov-kluby-rfpl-i-fnl-budut-platit-rfs-za-kazhdogo-legionera.
171. S. V. Alekseyev, *supra* n. 17, 2012, 316.

states that any reduction of the level of the rights and safeguards of professional sportsmen and coaches should be implemented by the LC.

268. The Government of the RF can also introduce limits by means of special annual quotas for foreign workers in certain economic sectors. Article 83(12) of LC RF lays down as a justified reason for dismissal of immigrant workers a government order to bring the number of foreign workers in line with the established quotas. It seems that such provisions may be in conflict with the international agreements concluded by the RF which guarantee equal treatment for nationals of other countries in the RF with regard to their rights to work. As mentioned above, Article 15(4) of the Russian Constitution establishes the priority over national law of the norms of international agreements signed by the RF. It should be however kept in mind that Russian Federation did not ratify a number of ILO conventions concerning the rights of the immigrants such as Migration for Employment Convention (1 July 1949, N. 97), Migrant Workers Convention (24 June 1975, N. 143) and the UN International Convention on the Protection of the Rights of all Migrant Workers and Members of their Families (18 December 1990).

269. At regional level it concluded an agreement with Belarus from 25 December 1998 'On Equal Rights of the Citizens',[172] the agreement with the Commonwealth of Independent States (CIS) countries on 15 April 1994 'On cooperation in the Sphere of Labour Migration and Social Protection of Migrant Workers',[173] and finally, an Agreement on Partnership and Cooperation Establishing a Partnership between the European Communities and their Member States, of one part, and the Russian Federation, of the other part (EC-Russia Partnership Agreement) from 24 June 1994 (Corfu, Greece).

270. In the connection with the latter one, mention should be made of the Simutenkov case,[174] sometimes compared to the Bosman case in terms of its scope, concerning the limits on international players. Simutenkov, employed in the time by the Spanish football club Deportivo Tenerife, contested the unlawful nature of the restrictions imposed on him as a citizen of a third country citing Article 23 of the above-mentioned EC-Russia Partnership Agreement prohibiting discrimination. In this case the European Court of Justice after quite a long examination of the case which lasted four years in 2005 ruled that the EC-Russia partnership agreement precludes the application to professional sportsmen of Russian nationality, lawfully employed by a club established in an EU Member State, of a rule established by sport federations limiting the participation of players from countries that are not members of the EEA agreement. In this way the court stated unacceptability of discrimination of Russian citizens by imposition of restrictions in employment relations based on nationality. It is important to add here that this ruling concerns only workers already legally residing and employed in the Member State and not entry and work permit requirements, which remain the prerogative of the Member State.[175] This case opened the possibility also

172. Ratified by the Federal Law from 1 May 1999 N. 89-FZ.
173. Ratified by the Federal Law from 24 Apr. 1995, N. 47-FZ.
174. Case C-265/03 *Igor Simutenkov v. Ministerio de Educacion y Cultura, Real Fedearcion Espagnola de Futbal* [2005] ECR I-5961.
175. F. Hendrickx, *The Simutenkov Case: Russian Players Are Equal to European Union Players*, Intl Sports L.J. 2005/3.

for other players in similar situations when their countries have bilateral agreements on cooperation with the EU claim discrimination in employment. Similar precedents existed also before the Simutenkov case when other Russian players such as Valery Karpin, Victor Onopko, Andrey Schevchenko, filed similar lawsuits in the Spanish courts.

271. Another consequence is that in base of reciprocity principle, in cases in which the nationals of the states with which the RF has similar bilateral international agreements and who wish to play in Russia, may file a claim for discrimination in employment. However since Russia does not recognize precedent any similar claim will be examined again in the Russian court which however may follow the logic of the Simutenkov case.[176]

272. From the economic point of view, the limits on legionnaires may result in an increase in costs for national players (or players with the Russian passport) comparable with the international level.

Moreover in order to bypass this ban, clubs often recourse to naturalization of the foreign players.

I. Work and Residence Permits

273. In Russia it is possible to hire foreign workers only if they are in possession of a work permit or work patent. The laws on immigration and foreign workforce in Russia are as follows:

- Chapter 50.1 of the Labour Code – (introduced by Federal Law of 01.12.14, N. 409-FZ);
- the Decree of the President of RF n. 2146 of 16 December 1993 'On the attraction and employment of foreign workers';
- the regulation of the Russian government no. 941 of 30 November 2002 'On the issuance of residence permits to foreign nationals';
- Federal Law N. 114-FZ of 15 August 1996 'On the modality of entrance and exit from the RF';
- Federal Law N. 115–FZ of 25 July 2002 'On the legal status of foreign citizens';
- Federal Law N. 110-FZ of 18 July 2006 'On amendments in the Federal Law on the legal status of foreign citizens';
- Federal Law N. 86 of 19 May 2010 'On amendments in the Federal Law on the Legal Status of Foreign Citizens';
- Federal N. 357-FZ Law of 24 November 2014 'On the amendments into the Federal Law 'On the legal status of foreign citizens' and other legislative acts of the RF;
- Federal Law N. 202-FZ of 29 June 2015 'On the amendments into the Federal law "On physical culture and sport" and Federal Law 115-FZ' On the legal status of foreign citizens'.

176. M. Prokopets, *Limits on Foreign Professional Players Competing in the Russian Federation: Problems and Prospects,* Int'l Sports L. J., 3-4, 36 (2009).

274. According to Law N. 115 foreign nationals have the same rights and obligations as Russian citizens in the absence of provisions in federal laws. A foreign national has the right to work on the RF territory after obtaining a work permit or a work patent.

275. From 2015 the citizens from the countries with which Russia has entry regimes without a visa (Ukraine, Uzbekistan, Tadzhikistan, Azerbaijan, Moldova) need to buy a special licence ('patent') to have the right to work. They have the right to stay in the RF territory for 90 days out of 180. Differently, the citizens from Kazakhstan, Belarus, Kirghizia, Armenia do not need neither a visa nor a patent as they are members of the Eurasian Economic Union (EEU) (2015).

276. The following categories of foreign workers are exempt from the requirement to obtain a work permit:

- those who have temporary residence permit for a period of 3–5 years, employed within diplomatic or consular bodies or international organizations;
- foreign journalists;
- students (on work experience during vacations) and teachers (with the exception of those in religious education).

277. Another exemption is granted for high-level professionals. Employers may hire high-level professionals who benefit from a number of advantages such as longer work permits, longer residence permits for the purpose of searching for a new job in case of termination of employment and so on. They also fall outside the quota system. Two criteria must be met to qualify as a high-level professional. First, it is necessary to have experience and outstanding achievements or skills in the sphere of activity, and second to receive an annual salary in Russia of not less than certain amount which is now diversified for the different categories of high-level professionals).[177]

278. Previously under law 115/2002-FZ the right to benefit from these exemptions was granted only to commercial, scientific research and certain other organizations. Since many sports bodies are non-profit organizations, it was unclear whether they could benefit from this rule. Now following the amendments introduced by the Federal Law of 29 June 2015 N. 202 (Article 20.4 of 'the Law on Sport' and Article 13.2 of the Federal Law 115/2002-FZ) the right to hire high-level professionals was extended also to sports organizations and All-Russian Sports Federations in accordance with the list of professions of foreign citizens and stateless persons approved by the Ministry of Sport.

177. Article 13(2) of the Federal Law on the Legal Status of Foreign Citizens N. 115-FZ. Before this threshold was RUB 2,000,000 rubbles. Now after the latest amendments to the art. 13(2) it varies for different categories of workers (the law does not specify this amount in particular for sportsmen so probably the general rule of the monthly salary of not less than RUB 167,000 will be applied).

279. In general according to the official data of Federal Immigration service of the RF during 2012 only 55,848 high-level foreign professionals (from 15,889,421 people) entered the RF territory. The share of sportsmen and coaches is only 3%.[178]

280. In order to obtain a work permit the employer must pay one month's salary and present the following documents:

- an application;
- a statement from the authorities regarding the need to hire foreign workers;
- a draft employment contract or other document confirming a preliminary employment agreement with the foreign worker.

281. The documents must be filed with the territorial employment agency of the corresponding administrative district, the regional office of employment and the immigration service of the Ministry of Internal Affairs.

282. A work permit is not required in the case of temporary transfers. To be considered a temporary transfer, the stay of the foreign national should not exceed one month, otherwise it will be deemed to be a standard employment contract. There are some exceptions (including some categories of sportsmen like instructors, senior coaches and the senior coach of the national team) but the duration cannot exceed forty calendar days over a two-month period, and the duration of the work activity cannot exceed ninety calendar days over a twelve-month period. Some exceptions exist for high-level professionals but they do not apply to all categories of sportsmen. Generally speaking the system is still highly restrictive from the point of view of the free movement of workers.[179]

283. The transfer system is also highly restrictive towards foreign workers as it limits their stay in regions other than the one for which the work permit was issued. Article 13(4) of the law on the legal status of foreign citizens prohibits them from performing work outside the region for which their work permit was issued.

284. Foreign sportsmen and coaches have the same rights and duties as national workers and their employment contract is governed by the LC RF and other legislative acts. However, Article 5(5) of the Federal Law on the Legal Status of Foreign Citizens lays down that the duration of the stay in the RF of a foreign citizen with an employment contract or civil law contract can be extended for the duration of the employment contract but for no more than one year. As a result, the work and residence permit of foreign players may be limited by the duration of their visa and (with few exceptions) it cannot exceed one year.

285. Foreign players are also covered by the general terms of termination of employment. There is, however, a special clause (Article 83(12) LCRF) which lays down an obligation to terminate the employment contract following a decision by the Government of the RF to bring the quota of foreign workers in line with the limits laid

178. http://www.fms.gov.ru/about/statistics/data/details/53595/ in the dissertation of R. Babaev, *The peculiarities of the legal regulation of labour of foreign citizens in the sphere of physical culture and sport in the RF*, Moscow, 2014, 26 (in Russian). (диссертация, Р. Бабаев, *Особенности правового регулирования труда иностранных граждан в сфере физической культуры и спорта в Российской Федерации*, М. 2014).

179. S. V. Alekseyev, *supra* n. 17, 2012, 334–335.

down by the government. However the mechanism of the termination of the contract for this reason is not specified by the Russian legislator which indicates only the obligation to respect the term established by the RF government in this regard so the employer has a certain margin of temporary flexibility. There is also no obligation for the employer to inform foreign workers on this decision (as it is included among the reasons not depending on the parties' will).[180]

286. In spite of the laws prohibiting discrimination, in practice it is difficult for sportsmen (and individuals in general) to prove discrimination in court due to the absence of the necessary mechanisms and due to judicial practice and culture. The legislation regulating the hiring of foreign players is still burdensome and in general creates bureaucratic obstacles to block the hiring of foreign workers especially in the case of sportsmen other than those at the highest level. It is still difficult for players to exercise their right to freedom of movement within the territory of Russia. The limit on 'legionnaires' may however be subject to appeal on the basis of its discriminatory nature and due to the implications of the *Simutenkov* case.

287. As for the termination of the employment contract because of the expiry of the work permit it is a responsibility of a club to ensure the player have a duly issued and, if necessary, renewed or prolonged residence permit. According to Article 18(4) of FIFA Regulations the validity of the contract cannot depend on the issuance of the residence permit. Obviously the player has an obligation to collaborate with the club and the omission of this duty will deprive the player of the right to present any claim. However the club is the body which has major opportunities to contact responsible national authorities and follow the established rules for the purpose of application of residence permit. The FUR Chamber adopted in general similar position. So in the case from 8 April 2011 N 86/11 regarding the claim of foreign player who asked a club a compensation for the termination of employment contracts without justified reason motivating it by the fact that his residence permit was going to expire the FUR Chamber cited Article 8(4) of the FIFA Regulations.[181]

288. Recently immigration laws in Russia have become more restrictive. So from 11 January 2015 more severe sanctions were introduced for immigrants who violate the terms of staying on the Russian territory. So in case the period of illegal stay on the Russian territory of a foreign citizen or a stateless person (*apatride*) exceeds 180 consecutive days but does not exceed 270 such persons will be prohibited the entrance in the RF for five years. If such a term is longer than 270 days, the prohibition of the entrance is ten years from the moment of the exit.[182] The immigration legislation foresees also the ban of entrance for three years for the foreign/stateless people who exceeded 90 days from 180 days of their total stay on the RF territory and for those who did not leave national territory within thirty days from the expiration of temporary residence permit.[183]

180. Babaev, 143–144.
181. M. Prokopets et al., *supra* n. 121, 2012, 89.
182. Federal Law from 31 Dec. 2014 N. 524-FZ amending Art. 27 of the Federal Law from 15 Aug. 1996 N 114-FZ 'On the regulation of the exit and entrance in the RF'.
183. Federal Law from 15 Aug. 1996 N 114-FZ.

289. Another restriction was introduced in the Law on Sport, Article 14(3.3) which includes among the conditions of receiving state accreditation by the All-Russian Sport Federation the absence of foreigners or stateless persons in its permanent bodies.[184]

So general restrictions imposed by the RF immigration laws concern:

- the necessity for a foreigner to have work permit or work patent;
- the limitation of his employment activity to the subject of the RF where work permit/patent was issue and to the type of activity specified in the work permit/ patent and difficulties to perform work even temporary outside this territory;
- prohibition to take certain professional positions or exercise certain activity or to visit certain geographical territories (which may be subject to specific authorization).

290. In general Russian immigration law, based on a quota system, lags significantly behind the economic, social and demographic needs of the country and it appears to be rigid, costly, burdensome and bureaucratic. Moreover quota system does not consider professional qualities of foreign workers and the correspondence between the necessity of the regional labour market and the accepted applications. Many industrialized countries have already abandoned the quota system in favour of more flexible schemes which permit to attract specialists and facilitate the opportunities for their employment and obtaining necessary documentation, (such as qualification certificates and diploma), without leaving the country.

184. Introduced by the Federal Law from 2 Dec.2012 N. 257-FZ.

Part III. Doping in Sport

291. Doping is not a recent phenomenon. It has been used even in ancient times as it is arguably an innate characteristic of humans to aspire victory and glory sometimes not caring about the price. Now, with the progressive commodification of sport, every year new records are broken and the expectations of professional sportsmen and women continue to rise.

292. As a result, a great number of sophisticated substances varying from anabolic steroids to psychotropic and genetic interventions are developed and it is difficult to keep such a process under control. Sometimes the line between prohibited substances and those that are permitted is a fine one. Moreover, many of these substances have different trade names in the national language[185] and the product labels do not always contain accurate information on the composition, making it more difficult to identify the presence of prohibited substances.

293. On the one hand, the anti-doping legislation and other measures to combat the use of doping are evolving, while on the other hand, the ways to circumvent anti-doping regulations become more and more innovative. Needless to say this harmful and unfair practice endangers both the health of competitors and the spirit of sport based on fair competition among equals. In an effort to tackle this problem the anti-doping measures include periodical updates of the prohibited substances/methods, while imposing sanctions not only on sportsmen and women but also on the support personnel including coaches, managers, sports doctors and any others potentially able to induce athletes to resort to doping.

294. In spite of its long history, the first doping tests were introduced by the IOC only in 1968, while a more coordinated campaign against doping was launched in 1998 when the first international conference on doping in sport was convened. Since then the anti-doping regulations have been subject to a number of changes. International norms aimed at possible convergence of rules in relation to doping have been adopted and are periodically updated.

295. Despite these efforts which have undoubtedly had an overall positive impact and contributed to the consolidation of national anti-doping provisions, each country continues to adopt its own anti-doping regulations. In some countries the use of doping is a criminal offence, while in others it is classified as an administrative offence or misdemeanour. International doping scandals normally result in changes in national anti-doping legislation towards stricter tests and sanctions. This was the

185. Consider the high profile case after the last doping scandal of *Meldonium*, also known as *Mildronate* (a non-specified substance included at S4 (Hormone and Metabolic Modulators) on the WADA prohibited list.

case after the scandal in 2015 in which many countries, and Russia in particular, found themselves facing serious financial and political implications.[186]

§1. Anti-doping Legislation

296. At the international level:

The current legislation on doping in Russia is based on international standards in particular:

- The World Anti-Doping Code (adopted 3 March 2003 at the World Conference on the Fight against Doping in Sport);[187]
- Anti-Doping Convention ETS N 135, Strasbourg, 16 November 1989;[188]
- Copenhagen Declaration on Anti-Doping in Sport (2003);
- International Convention against Doping in Sport 2005.[189]

297. The main sources of the international anti-doping programme include:

- The WADA Code
- International standards
- Models of best practice

298. At the national level:

The legal basis of anti-doping measures is to be found in different normative acts varying from federal and regional laws to by-laws (legislative decrees and orders of the RF government, Ministry of Sport) and general anti-doping rules. The main normative acts in this field are:

- RF Constitution
- Labour Code RF (Chapter 54.1)
- Order of Goskomsport [190] 'On the organisation of anti-doping measures in sport in RF', 20 October 2003, No. 837

186. Following the publication in 2014 of the first McLaren Report and anti-doping investigations by the MOC and the World Anti-Doping Agency (WADA), a great number of Russian athletes were excluded from the Olympic games in Rio (2016) and all of them from Paralympics. The medals won by Russian athletes during the Sochi Olympics were cast into doubt and the general reputation of Russia on the international sport arena was seriously damaged. *See* https://www.wada-ama.org/en/media/news/2016-12/wada-publishes-independent-mclaren-investigation-report-part-ii
187. The new version of the Anti-doping Code was adopted on 15 Nov. 2013, 2013 in Johannesburg entering into force on 1 Jan. 2015. It introduces stricter sanctions for sportsmen and women accused of using doping http://www.minsport.gov.ru/press-centre/news/23278/.
188. The USSR joined this Convention 28 Dec. 1990 by means of regulation N 1351 (entering into force for RF 1 Apr. 1991).
189. Adopted at thirty-third UNESCO Session Paris, (October 2005), ratified by the Russian Federation by means of the Federal Law of 27 Dec. 2006 N 240-FZ.
190. Goskomsport (state committee of sport) transformed into the Ministry of Sport in 2012.

- Federal Law of 27 December 2006 N. 240-FZ 'On Ratification of the International Convention against Doping in Sport' 2005
- Federal Law 'On Physical Culture and Sport RF' of 4 December 2007 N. 329-FZ (Law on Sport)
- Article 234, 230.1 and 230.2[191] of the Penal Code RF (1996)
- Article 3.11, 6.18[192] Code of Administrative Offences RF (2001)
- Order of the Ministry of Sport RF of 13 May 2009 N. 293 'On the approval of the procedure of doping test performance'
- Order of the Ministry of Sport of 27 May 2010 N. 525 'On Anti-doping Support of RF Teams by Federal Budget'
- Government Decree of 11 November 2010 N 884 'Modality of Import on the RF Territory of Samples for Doping tests'
- Federal Law of 21 November 2011 N. 323-FZ 'On the Foundations for Health of the RF Citizens'
- Order of the Ministry of Sport of 17 December 2015 N. 1194 'On the Approval of Substances or Methods Prohibited in Sport'
- Federal Law of 22 November 2016 N. 296-FZ 'On Amendments to the Federal Law 'On sport' in part concerning the regulation of high-level professional sport'
- Order of the Ministry of Sport of 9 August 2016, N. 947[193] 'On the adoption of anti-doping rules'
- Federal Law of 22 November 2016 N. 392-FZ 'On the amendments to the Penal Code RF and the Code of Criminal Procedure of the Russian Federation (on stricter liability for violation of anti-doping rules)'.

299. Following the amendments enacted in 2010,[194] the Law on Sport (4 December 2007 N. 329-FZ) introduced an official definition of doping and regulated many important doping-related aspects. Under Article 26, doping is a violation of anti-doping rules including the use (or attempted use) of prohibited substances or methods listed in the periodically updated World Anti-Doping Code. In addition to persons, the use of doping is prohibited for animals taking part in competitions. The provisions of this Law specify the procedure for doping tests including test planning, sample collection and storage, transportation, laboratory analysis and after-test procedures as well as provisions in relation to court hearings and appeals (Article 26(5). Under Article 26(8) the general anti-doping measures include:

191. Federal Law of 22 Nov. 2016 N. 392-FZ 'On the amendments in the Penal Code RF and the Code of Criminal Procedure of the Russian Federation(on stricter liability for violation of anti-doping rules)' introduces new Arts 230. 1 and 230.2.
192. Art 6.18 of the Code of Administrative offenses 'Breach of the Provisions on Doping Prevention in Sport and Fight against Doping Established by the Legislation on Physical Education and Sport' was introduced by the Federal Law 413 from 6 Dec. 2011.
193. Repealing the previous Ministry of Sport Order 'On the adoption of anti-doping rules' from 18 Jun. 2015, N. 638. The new text reproduces the analogous text of the latest version of the WADA Code.
194. Introduced by the Federal Law of 07.05.2010 N. 82-FZ, (the previous version did not provide a definition of doping but limited itself to prohibiting its use and listed some measures in this regard).

- administration of doping tests;
- accountability of sportsmen and women, coaches and other persons involved in sport activity for the violation of anti-doping rules;
- prevention of the use of doping means and methods;
- appropriate training of the personnel responsible for anti-doping tests;
- inclusion in special educational programmes of sport and physical culture institutions of modules explaining possible harm doping may produce for the health of the individual and responsibility for the violation of anti-doping rules;
- doping prevention campaigns in the mass media;
- scientific anti-doping research;
- promotion of scientific research in relation to the development of methods enabling sportsmen effective recovery;
- accountability of physical culture organizations, sportsmen and women, coaches, doctors and other stakeholders for the violation of the rules on obligatory anti-doping tests;
- enhancing of international cooperation in the prevention of doping.

300. Article 26 of the law further specifies the anti-doping measures to be implemented by the stakeholders involved in sport such as the federal executive governmental body, the All-Russian sport federations and professional leagues, the organizers of sport events and the Russian anti-doping agency.

301. In particular, the federal government executive body should approve All-Russia anti-doping rules, list of prohibited substances and doping test procedures. Moreover it is authorized to take decisions on the exclusion of All-Russia Sports Federation from the register of accredited sport federations in the case of violation of anti-doping rules.

302. The All-Russian Sports Federations and professional leagues must adopt measures on anti-doping and impose sanctions (including disqualification) on the sportsmen and women accused of doping and any persons who induce/coerce the sportsmen and women to use them. Moreover, they are required to publish or place on their internet websites national anti-doping rules and anti-doping rules approved by the international sport federations in relation to the kind of sport concerned. They must provide the national anti-doping agency with all necessary information concerning sportsmen and women testing during in- and out-of-competition period, collaborate in doping tests, apply sanctions for the breach of anti-doping rules, providing information about the applied sanctions to federal governmental executive body and regional executive bodies, national anti-doping agency and international federation of the kind of sport concerned.

303. The organizers of sport events must ensure effective doping tests during sports events, collaborate in testing athletes during these events and comply with the anti-doping legislation. If the organizer of the event is the All-Russian Sport Federation, it is required to respect Article 26(10) of the Law on Sport. In case of violations of anti-doping norms the organizer can be cancelled from the register of All-Russian accredited regional sport federations.

304. In the case of breach of anti-doping norms national sports federations may be suspended from their membership in the international sports federations. This means it is not possible for the suspended federation to enter their sportsmen and women for international sports competitions.

305. Following the recent doping scandal this happened with the Russian Athletic Federation (RusAF) and Russian Paralympic Committee RPC) whose respective membership of the International Association of Athletic Federation (IAAF) and in the International Paralympic Committee (IPC) was suspended.

306. As a result All-Russian athletes and Paralympic sportsmen and women were excluded from taking part in the Rio Olympic games. However, unlike the IPC, the IAAF provided in their competition regulations an additional clauses[195] permitting the participation of 'clean' sportsmen and women in the Rio Olympics with the status of a 'neutral athlete', i.e., without the right to represent Russia. Both cases were contested by the national federations involved in the CAS[196] which upheld the decisions to suspend Russian teams from the Olympics.

307. In response to the appellants' claims that in this way innocent sportsmen and women suffered a sort of 'collective punishment' the CAS clarified that the ban imposed on Russian sportsmen and women taking part in the Rio Olympics was 'a necessary consequence of the sanction imposed on the national federation for failure to live up to its obligations' (clause 80 of the CAS decision 2016/O/4684) while 'the effect of innocent athletes, which is unfortunate, is overweighed by the benefits of retaining public confidence in the integrity of intentional competition and preventing other athletes from being cheated out of the medals, prize, money and glory they deserve' (clause 92 of the CAS decision 2016/O/4684).

308. Anti-doping agency at national level – RUSADA.[197]

309. To ensure effective doping control of the athletes taking part in the Olympics and generally in support of the fight against doping, an independent national anti-doping organization RUSADA was established in 2008 at the initiative of the Federal Agency for Physical Culture and Sport in compliance with the WADA Code, the UNESCO International Convention against Doping in Sport and Article 26.1 of the 'Law on Sport'. In May 2008 RUSADA was accredited by the World Anti-Doping Agency as a National Anti-Doping Organization and placed on the WADA list of anti-doping organizations.

310. In 2009 WADA approved the National Anti-Doping Rules adopted by RUSADA as compliant with the WADA Code. Throughout the period RUSADA cooperated with the World Anti-Doping Agency, national anti-doping organizations of other countries and a number of international and national sport federations. In 2009 RUSADA joined the ANADO. RUSADA also cooperates with regional sport institutions and Russian Sports Federations.

311. According to Article 20.5 of the WADA Code and Article 26.1 of the Law on Sport, RUSADA carries out the following tasks:

195. On 17 Jun. 2016 the IAAF Council passed an amendment to the competition rules, namely Rule 22.1.A which provides a definition of 'neutral athletes' and on 23 Jun. 2016 the IAAF provided guidelines concerning the application of Rule 22.1A.
196. CAS 2016/O/4684 The Russian Olympic Committee (ROC) v. The International Association of Athletics Federations (IAAF); CAS 2016/A/4745 Russian Paralympic Committee v. International Paralympic Committee.
197. www.rusada.ru.

- plans, coordinates, controls and enhances doping tests procedures;
- collaborates with other relevant national organizations and agencies and other anti-doping organizations;
- encourages reciprocal testing between national anti-doping organizations;
- promotes anti-doping research;
- strongly pursues all potential anti-doping rule violations within its jurisdiction including investigation into whether sportsmen support personnel or other persons may have been involved in each case of doping and to ensure proper enforcement of consequences;
- promotes anti-doping education;
- carries out an automatic investigation of sports support personnel within its jurisdiction in the case of any anti-doping rule violation by a minor and of any support personnel providing support for more than one athlete found to have committed an anti-doping rule violation;
- closely cooperates with WADA in investigations conducted by WADA.

For these purposes RUSADA carries out in- and out-of-competition testing, and target testing, including carrying out orders from the international sports federations. The RUSADA personnel includes 23 doping test officers working full-time and almost 50 doping test officers working in the regions, providing more than 20,000 samples collected annually. Doping test officers are re-accredited and audited annually.

In compliance with the WADA Code and International Standards, RUSADA coordinates two independent departments:

(1) Therapeutic Use Exemption Committee (TUEC), which is in charge of looking into Therapeutic Use Exemption requests.
(2) Anti- Doping Disciplinary Committee, set up to hold fair impartial hearings for athletes committing anti-doping rule violations.

312. RUSADA works in close cooperation with the World Anti-Doping Agency, international anti-doping organizations and a number of international sport federations in educational and testing programmes.

313. Anti-doping obligations are laid down also in other normative acts such as the Labour Code (Article 348(2), the Regulations on the Status and Transfer of Players (for football) and regulations of other sport federations. They include an obligation to ensure that athletes do not use prohibited substances/methods, regularly take doping tests and so on. In addition they include an obligation for employers to provide information about the location of sportsmen and women for doping testing.

314. The following actions are classified as violation of anti-doping rules (Article 2 of the Russian anti-doping rules):[198]

(1) Presence of prohibited substances or their metabolites or markers in the athlete's sample.

198. Order of Ministry of Sport of 9 Aug. 2016, N. 947. A similar list is contained in Art 26(3) of the Law on Sport.

(2) Use or attempted use by the sportsman or woman of a prohibited method or substance.
(3) Refusal or failure to submit a sample after the athlete has been notified, as authorised in the applicable anti-doping rules (unless a valid justification for such actions is provided).
(4) Failures or omissions consisting of any combination of three missed tests and (or) filing failures, as defined in the International Standard for Testing and Investigations, over a 12-month period by an athlete in a Registered Testing Pool.
(5) Falsification or attempt of falsification in any sphere of doping tests.
(6) Possession of prohibited substances and materials.
(7) Trafficking or attempted trafficking in prohibited substances or materials.
(8) Administration or attempted administration to any athlete in-competition of any prohibited substance or prohibited method, or administration or attempted administration to any athlete out-of-competition of any prohibited substance or any prohibited method that is prohibited out-of-competition.
(9) Complicity.
(10) Prohibited association.

315. The procedure for obligatory anti-doping testing is laid down by the Ministry of Sport.[199] The Ministry of Sport of Russia and its jurisdictional bodies with other sports organizations are required to implement the policy against doping on the entire territory of the RF in- and out-of-competition. Some important procedural measures in this regard are listed in the order of the Ministry of Sport 'On the organisation of anti-doping measures in sport in RF' dated 20 October 2003, No. 837. Pursuant to its provisions the rights of selection, codification and transportation of the doping tests are assigned only to the personnel of the department of anti-doping tests of the Centre of Sports Department. At least two persons are required to be present. Moreover, they must have special qualifications and possess a certificate testifying their status as of specialists in anti-doping tests.

316. The following anti-doping testing procedure is laid down:

(1) Anti-doping testing is carried out in accordance with the plan for in- and out-of-competition doping tests established by the Ministry of Sport and requests by the All-Russian Sports Federations for supplementary anti-doping tests.
(2) Any sportsmen and women in the national Russian teams, sportsmen and women in sports academies, and Olympic reserve players during training can be subject to out-of-competition doping tests under the closed schedule.

The following organizations have the right to carry out out-of-competition testing:

- WADA;
- International Olympic Committee (IOC) or International Paralympics Committee (IPC);

199. Order of Goskomsport (now Ministry of Sport) 'On the organization of anti-doping measures in sport in RF', 20 Oct. 2003, No. 837; Order of Ministry of Sport RF of 13 May 2009 N. 293 'On the approval of the procedure of doping test performance'.

- International federation on the sport concerned;
- Russian Ministry of Sport;
- National anti-doping organization of a country of the actual location of the sportsman or woman.

(3) The collaborator of the anti-doping committee is a member of the organizing committee or main panel of judges for the sport competitions.
(4) The panel of judges for the sport competitions must provide from one to three judges responsible for the appearance of the athlete at the doping test point.
(5) The main panel of judges for the sport competitions must ensure the representatives of anti-doping tests of the starting and final protocols and inform them about the performance of the sportsmen and women.
(6) The organizers of competitions are required to ensure all the conditions for doping tests.
(7) The organizers are obliged to:

- prepare the site for the work of the anti-doping committee according to the established requirements;
- ensure the conditions for anti-doping tests and sample storage, and exclude any possibility of their opening, theft, or substitution and where necessary, ensure protection of the premises of doping tests by the law enforcement agencies.
- provide transportation for the staff of anti-doping committee and sportsmen and women staying at the doping test point;
- provide the staff of the anti-doping committee with permits providing access to all facilities, including locker rooms and changing facilities, and access to competition sites (finish, platform, field, track, ring) as well as permits for cars with an indication of the nearest parking facilities to the doping test point.

§2. Procedure of Doping Tests

317. The procedure of anti-doping tests consists of gathering two samples (A and B) from the sportsmen and women, their analysis and supply of the test results for sample A and control tests of sample B. In the case of violation, sanctions are applied. The representatives of doping test bodies and federations are required to inform the athletes, coaches, medical staff and other interested persons about the procedural rules.

318. According to the general regulations, doping tests are obligatory for prize winners and for other competitors, chosen at random (drawing lots). In track-and-field athletics, skiing, figure skating, ski jumping, biathlons, mountain skiing, shooting sports, pentathlon, cycling, fencing, weightlifting, swimming and diving doping tests are required for those winning the first, second and third prizes or one to six (shooting) and one or two competitors chosen at random (drawing lots). In team sports one or two competitors from each team (depending on the number of team members), winning the first three prizes, are selected; in figure skating one competitor from the couple (at random); in bobsleigh and luge either the whole team or one or two competitors at random from the teams winning the main prizes; in rowing and sailing the teams winning the first, second and third prizes and one team at random. Among the members of these teams, one or two competitors are chosen by lot; in gymnastics (main programme): two competitors (male and female) winning the first and third prize or the first and second prize. In free programmes the sportsmen are chosen by lot. In the final the same principle as in the main programme is applied; in team sports: one or two competitors from each team are chosen by lot. In the case of shooting and pentathlon (including archery) an obligatory alcohol test for 50% or all the competitors is also required.

319. The regulations for doping tests are agreed with the representatives of the national or international federations (depending on whether the competitions are held at national or international level). During the competitions, the competitors may be tested several times. The competition regulations are determined at a technical meeting of the teams and judges and they cannot be changed for the entire period of the competition (except in cases when the amendments are made by the main judge panel or representatives of international sport federations). At the discretion of the main panel, competitors whose behaviour or inadequate reactions or strange appearance raise suspicions may be tested.

320. The selection of the competitors for random testing is made by the staff member of the anti-doping body with the participation of the representatives of the federation. The results of the random selection (drawing lots) are reflected in the special protocol and are kept confidential until the end of the competition. The selected competitors must be informed after the competition about the time and place of the doping tests. The competitor is obliged to appear at the doping test point with a valid identity document within an hour of the notification being handed over and signed by the athlete. Failure to appear or refusal to undergo a test counts as evidence of the use of doping and the relative sanctions are applied. Also the refusal of a competitor to sign the notification, any delay in turning up for testing or any attempt at falsification of the test at any stage are sanctioned.

321. In addition to the competitors, staff members of the anti-doping body, staff at the doping test point, representatives of the sports federation, representatives of the international federation, the team doctor or team representative and interpreter may be present at the doping test but as a rule the press are not allowed to attend.

322. The competitor is not permitted to leave the doping test point. In case of the sportsman's invitation at the awards ceremony, the collected sample test is sealed and the competitor's representative remains at the doping test point in the competitor's absence. The testing is carried out behind closed doors and persons accompanying the competitor are prohibited from entering.

323. The officer in charge of the test point must demonstrate to the competitor and the accompanying person that the test tubes are correctly sealed and marked. The officer is then required to record in the minutes the code number and list of medicines taken by the competitor within the last three days and demonstrate to the competitor and his/her representative that the code number of the test tubes correspond to the code number recorded in the minutes. The competitor, his/her representative and the staff member of the anti-doping body are required to sign the minutes. One copy is to be given to the competitor.

324. The sealed test tubes are then sent by special delivery in a special container suitable for transport to the laboratory with receipt of delivery. At the same time as the transport takes place the minutes with the respective codes and information on any medicines taken by the competitor are sent. The minutes with data on the competitor and codes of the test tubes are sealed and are kept in a safe box until the results of the analysis. All the data are computerized.

325. Physical and chemical analysis of the samples is carried out in the WADA accredited anti-doping laboratory according to international standards. The analysis should be carried out within 72 hours of receipt of the sample, and in case of international competitions within 48 hours. In some cases delays are allowed but no more than five days. Positive test results are reported to the Minister of Sport, the Director of the Anti-Doping Commission of the Ministry of Sport and the President of the Sports Federation concerned.

326. Also the competitor must be informed about positive results and about his or her rights. In this case the competitor has the right to ask to examine sample B. In the absence of such a request within seven days of notification the federation informs the Anti-Doping Commission of the refusal of the competitor to analyse sample B and thus the use of doping is confirmed. The competitor and/or his/her representative have the right to be present at the opening of sample B if they asked to examine it. Moreover, according to international standards, the athlete has the right to receive copies of documents concerning analysis of samples A and B.

327. If the result of testing of sample B does not confirm the results on sample A, the overall analysis is considered to be negative.

328. After the notification of positive test results, the federation must conduct its own investigation and inform the competitor of the outcome.

329. After the notification about the positive test results on sample A the competitor is suspended from competitions until the decision on sanctions is taken. If the testing of sample B (which must be conducted within seven days of the request from the competitor) confirms the positive doping results of sample A, it is considered to be final and the sanctions according to the WADA Code are applied to the competitor.[200]

§3. Sanctions

330. Under the amended anti-doping rules, any competitor whose use of doping has been duly demonstrated is subject to four years' disqualification[201] and in the case of a third occurrence (except in cases when in the previous test no fault or negligence of the competitor was found) to lifelong disqualification (Article 10.7.1. of the Rules).

331. In general the sanctions have become more complex but at the same time more fine-tuned and provide several possibilities to mitigate them. For instance in cases of less serious infringements (such as violation of the means of communication of the location by the competitor (Article 2.4 Russian anti-doping rules) a two-year

200. Y. V. Stukalova, *supra* n. 45, 2009.
201. The previous version of WADA Code provided a two-year term.

term is applied with the possibility of further reduction up to one year in relation to the degree of fault. These measures are not applied to competitors who intentionally provide misleading information to avoid doping tests.

332. Also in the case of the prompt and voluntary admission by the competitor of the violation of anti-doping rules, according to Article 10.2.1 and 10.3.1 of the Rules (establishing four-year term), after WADA and RUSADA consent, the disqualification period may be reduced by up to two years depending on the seriousness of the violation and the fault.

333. The period of disqualification may also be reduced if a competitor can prove that it was not his/her fault or negligence or he/she provides significant assistance to the bodies involved in doping crimes investigation and/or voluntarily discloses doping violation information. The final decision will be taken by the anti-doping organization requesting the disqualification.

334. Normally no more than three-quarters of the disqualification period may be changed. In the case of lifelong disqualification, the reduction period cannot be less than eight years. However, in exceptional cases at its discretion WADA can cancel the disqualification term entirely and not require the return of the prize money.

335. The new version of the rules provides that more severe sanctions up to lifelong disqualification as well as penal and administrative sanctions should be applied to the support personnel for cases when minors are involved as such violations are considered to be particularly serious.

336. The disqualification rulings may be appealed in the Court of Appeal (Chapter XIII of the Rules, Article 13(2)- 13(6). The term to present an appeal to CAS is twenty-one days from the date of the receipt of the decision by the appellant.

337. The competitor should be subject to anti-doping out-of-competition testing before the termination of the disqualification and the return to the sport activity. No financial sanction can influence, decrease or annul the disqualification. In the case of summing up of different sanctions, the financial sanction is the first to be cancelled if the overall set of sanctions represent an excessive burden for the competitor. In case of team sports if more than two players are accused of doping the whole team is sanctioned in addition to the culpable individuals.

338. A landmark recent case in this regard is the CAS decision in *Sharapova.*[202]

Following a CAS decision, the period of suspension of Maria Sharapova was reduced by nine months, from two years to fifteen months, beginning on 26 January 2016. This decision modified the previous one handed down by the Independent Tribunal appointed by the ITF which found her in violation of anti-doping rules for the use of Mildronate that was on the WADA prohibited list, disqualified her results at the 2016 Australian Open, and imposed a two-year suspension period while delivering the following decision:

> 'The contravention of the anti-doping rule was not intentional as Ms Sharapova did not appreciate that Mildronate contained a substance prohibited from 1 January 2016. However she does bear sole responsibility for the contravention, and very significant fault, in failing to take any steps to check whether the continued use of this medicine was permissible. If she had not concealed her use

202. CAS 2016/A/4643 *Maria Sharapova v. International Tennis Federation.*

of Mildronate from the anti-doping authorities, members of her own support team and the doctors whom she consulted, but had sought advice, then the contravention would have been avoided. She is the sole author of her misfortune.'

339. Sharapova appealed this decision, claiming the unintentional use of this medicine not with the aim of enhancing her performance. She asked the panel to reduce her ineligibility period on the basis of 'non significant fault' (NSF*).* The CAS panel considered the pubic admission of the use of the medicine by the athlete and its unintentional use. However, it rejected the request to apply the NSF principle considering that the player 'bore some degree of fault for the failure to make sure that the substance contained in a product that she had been taking over a long period remained in compliance with the anti-doping rules'. Thus the court stated that her fault was greater than NSF but less than significant fault and ruled that fifteen months would be an appropriate sanction in this case.

340. In the case of violation the results of any competition are annulled and the competitors forfeit their prizes and medals (Article 10.1 of the Rules). Under Article 10.9 of the Rules concerning the allocation of CAS cost awards and forfeit prize money, the financial resources are first allocated to CAS, in second place to the other competitors if it is provided in the rules of the international federation concerned, and lastly they are allocated for the reimbursement of RUSADA expenses.

341. A disqualified person has no right to take part in competitions (Article 10.11 of the Rules). In the case of a violation of this provision, the results of the competitions will be annulled and a new suspension period equal in length to the original one will be added to the end of the original period. When support personnel or other persons assist disqualified persons in committing the violation of ineligibility period, the sanctions under Article 2.9 of the Rules (Complicity) will be applied.

342. Any person found to be in violation of the doping rules also loses state funding related to sport including the right to the monthly president bursary.[203] The sportsmen will not have a right for a president bursary for two years after the end of the disqualification period.[204]

343. Following the new version of the WADA Code, the Russian anti-doping rules extend the term of prescription of the doping crime from eight to ten years.[205]

344. Disqualifications are subject to public disclosure (Article 14.3 of the Rules) by the national anti-doping agency only after the notification to the competitor and no later than twenty days after the final appeal decision (except in cases when minors are involved).

203. Decree of the President of RF from 31 Mar. 2011 N. 368 'On bursaries of the president of Russian Federation to sportsmen, coaches and other specialists of Russian teams for sports included in the programme of Olympic, Paralympics and deaf Olympic games and champions'.
204. Amendments to the Decree of the President of RF from 31 Mar. 2011 N. 368 introduced by the President Decree from 15 Jul. 2017 N.321.
205. Order of Ministry of Sport from 30 Dec. 2014 N. 1107 'Implementing new requirements following the introduction of the new version of the World anti-doping code becoming effective from 1 Jan. 2015'. Art. XVII of Russian anti-doping rules.

§4. Burden of Proof

345. The burden of proof of doping-related violations is laid upon the national anti-doping agencies, in our case, upon RUSADA.

346. According to Article 3.1 of the Rules: 'this standard of proof in all cases is greater than a mere balance of probability but less than proof beyond a reasonable doubt. Where the Code places the burden of proof upon the athlete or other person alleged to have committed an anti-doping rule violation to rebut a presumption or establish specified facts or circumstances, the standard of proof shall be by a balance of probability'.

347. This means in practice that, unlike other branches of the law, where the main criterion is the presumption of innocence, in the case of sport reasonable suspicion is sufficient. The burden of proof is shifted to the athlete who is required to prove his/her innocence.

348. In addition to the sanctions laid down in the Russian anti-doping rules in accordance with the WADA Code, additional sanctions are to be found in the Penal Code RF (1996), the Code of Administrative Offences RF (2001) and the Labour Code RF (2001).

349. In addition to the existing rights, Article 38.11 of the Labour Code RF establishes the right of the employer to dismiss the athlete in case of even one instance of abuse of anti-doping rules on condition this violation was duly confirmed by the authorized anti-doping organization.

350. Article 6.18 of the Russia Code of Administrative Offences establishes that for violations by the support personnel of the rules of anti-doping legislation regarding coercion or other forms of inducement of sportsmen to use doping or complicity in its use a disqualification from one to two years, and up to three years in cases in which the violation concerns a minor.

351. Following the recent doping scandal involving a significant number of Russian athletes, after heated debate, the Russian State Duma approved Federal Law of 22 November 2016 N. 392-FZ 'On the amendments to the Penal Code RF and the Code of Criminal Procedure of the Russian Federation (on stricter liability for violation of anti-doping rules)' laying down penal responsibility for breaches of anti-doping legislation on the part of support personnel.

352. In particular, two more articles are included in the Penal Code (Article 230.1 'Provisions on sportsmen using prohibited substances and/or methods' and Article 230.2 'Use in regard of the sportsman of prohibited substances and/or methods').

353. New legal provisions increase the sanctions for the violation of doping rules which include fines, imprisonment and disbarment from certain professional positions or from carrying out professional activity in sport. Under Article 230.1, provisions[206] on sportsmen and women using doping, the fines for individuals amount to RUB 300,000 or six months' salary (or other income for this period). It may also result in imprisonment up to one year with or without disbarment from certain

206. Comprising any deliberate actions favouring the use by the sportsmen of prohibited substances/methods, which may consist of deceit, persuasion, advice, information on prohibited substances/methods or eliminating obstacles for their use.

professional positions or from carrying out certain professional activity up to three years.

354. The same crime committed by a group of persons as a result of preliminary conspiracy, in relation to a minor(s), under blackmail, violence or threat of its use, is punished with a fine up to RUB 500,000, one year's salary (or other income for this period), with or without disbarment from certain professional positions or from carrying out certain professional activities for up to four years. If such actions result in the death of the sportsman or other serious consequences, three years' imprisonment is established with or without disbarment from certain professional positions or from carrying out certain professional activity for up to five years, or forced labour up to three years and/or disbarment from certain professional positions or from carrying out certain professional activities up to five years.

355. Article 230(2) regulating the use by a sportsman or woman of prohibited substances and/or methods is punished by a one million rouble fine, or two years' salary (or other income for this period), one or two years' imprisonment with or without disbarment from certain professional positions or from carrying out certain professional activities for up to four years, or forced labour for up to three years with or without disbarment from certain professional positions or from carrying out certain professional activities for up to five years.

356. If such actions result in the death of the sportsman or woman, or other serious consequences, three years' imprisonment is provided with or without disbarment from certain professional positions or from carrying out certain professional activities for up to five years, or forced labour for up to three years with or without disbarment from certain professional positions or from carrying out certain professional activities for up to five years.

357. The adoption of this law divided the opinion of legal scholars and other sport stakeholders.[207] Some consider these measures reasonable and legitimate, while others underline their predominantly political character, claiming that administrative sanctions would be sufficient. In their view, the Penal Code RF already contains sanctions for the use and sale of narcotic psychotropic substances and others[208] which could have been simply extended or integrated with the specific clauses in relation to doping. It would seem that both critics and defendants are right in part and, as often in these cases, the most reasonable interpretation lies somewhere in the middle.

358. Stricter sanctions are necessary to discourage violations of anti-doping provisions. On the contrary, it is evident that they are not a panacea and a complex approach combining preventive and punitive measures as well as incentives for honest competitors would be more appropriate. Moreover, a better coordination of legal norms in various spheres relating to sport (for instance general medicine, advertising) and effective anti-doping educational campaigns appears to be necessary for the eradication of doping.

207. http://www.zakonia.ru/theme/zakon-o-dopinge-spasenie-sporta-ot-zarazy-ili-lishnjaja-nagruzka-dlja-sudov-10-11-2016 (in Russian).

208. Art 235 PC RF lays down responsibility for unlawful pharmaceutical activity; Art 230 PC RF punishes the induction to use narcotic and psychotropic substances; Art. 234 PC RF regulates the illegal turnover of strong or poisonous substances for the purpose of sale.

§5. Sport Agents

359. Federal Law N. 396-FZ off 22 November 2016, amended the Law 'On Sport' (Law 329-FZ of 4.12.2007) with a new Article 19(3) on sports agents. Following these amendments, Article 20(2) of the Law on Sport defines a sports agent as 'a natural or legal person who by means of legal or other actions carries out activity with the aim of finding employment for players and coaches in professional sports clubs'.

Pursuant to Article 19(3) agents have the right to conclude agency contracts with players, coaches and professional sport clubs under Russian law, the norms of the All-Russian Sports Federations and professional leagues in conformity with the Law on Sport and the regulations of the international sports federations. They can resolve disputes in the courts of arbitration for sport pursuant to Russian legislation, or use pretrial procedures such as mediation.

Agents are obliged to defend the interests of the sportsman or woman, coach or club in good faith, to abstain from gambling or betting in bookmakers' agencies for the sport they represent, to comply with the code of ethics and to fulfil other obligations laid down by law.

Sports agents are required to be accredited with the All-Russia Sports Federation responsible for the sport represented by the agent. Non-accredited agents are prohibited. The accreditation is required to contain the following information:

- Terms and procedure of the accreditation
- Duties of the sports agents
- The duration of accreditation which cannot exceed five years
- Provisions in the contracts with the agents including maximum duration
- Reasons and procedure for the application of sanctions such as the suspension or revocation of accreditation
- Procedure for notification by the professional sports league of the sports federation of the suspension or revocation of accreditation in cases in which the accreditation is carried out jointly by the league and the federation.
- In addition the following requirements apply:
- Publication by accreditation organizations on their websites of the list of accredited agents as well as information about the suspension or revocation of accreditation.
- Supervision by the accreditation organizations of the activity of their agents.
- Prohibition on payment to for agency services by athletes and players below the age of 16.

§6. Football Intermediaries

360. In the past two years the activity of football intermediaries has been subject to radical changes following the corresponding FIFA reform in this field. The Regulations on Working with Intermediaries (2015)[209] were aligned with the corresponding FIFA Regulations.[210] They abrogated the former regulations on football intermediaries N.

209. Decree of the Executive Committee of FUR 164/4, 30 Mar. 2015.
210. Circular n. 1417 Zurich, 30 Apr. 2014.

131[211] which ceased to be valid as from 1 April 2015. Under the new provisions (Regulations 2015) the agents' licensing system was abrogated and all licences issued by the RFU became null and void.

In 2017 a new version of the Regulations on Working with Intermediaries was adopted[212] in conformity with the Federal Law N. 396-FZ of 22 November 2016. The new regulations entered in force on 15 May 2017 repealing those adopted in 2015 and introducing a number of important changes. They apply to all agency contracts concluded after this date. All contracts concluded before this date with the persons without FUR accreditation will be valid only in relation to their right to remuneration if such a right was in place before this date. In cases in which an intermediary received accreditation by 15 June 2017, the contracts stipulated before 15 May 2017 corresponding to the accreditation category and in compliance with the new regulations (2017) can be recognized by the FUR and registered by the Commission within seven working days of receipt of accreditation by the intermediary without the application of sanctions by the sports federations. Consequently under these contracts the intermediaries have the right to carry out activities in relation to the representation of sportsmen/coaches interests regarding their employment contract/transfers. Disputes regarding contracts stipulated before 15 May 2017 do not fall under the jurisdiction of the FUR (Article 20 of the 2017 Regulations).

According to Article 1 of the regulations, intermediaries (sport agents) are sports professionals and they can be a natural or a legal person (including foreign nationals) representing the interests of the clubs (including foreign clubs), players or coaches either free of charge or for remuneration for their negotiations aimed at concluding transfer contracts, or concluding, changing or terminating employment contracts. Under these regulations, intermediaries are sport agents according to the Federal Law 329-FZ of 04.12.2007 'Law on Sport'.

The regulations (2015) introduced a number of important changes. First they cancelled the licensing system thus transferring control over the intermediaries' activity from FIFA to the national federations. Under the regulations (2015) federations were required to register the intermediary upon presentation of the required documents (Article 5 of the regulations (2015)). The new version of the regulations (2017) makes the accreditation procedure more complicated from an economic and a procedural point of view.

Pursuant to Article 4 of the new regulations, since 1 January 2017 intermediaries have been obliged to pay per PRO category RUB 10,000,000 to obtain accreditation. From the second year the fee for the PRO category becomes RUB 3,000,000 annually. These fees vary by category (A- RUB 2,000,000 plus 5% of the agent's gross income for the respective year; B- RUB 500,000 plus 5% of the intermediary's gross income for the respective year, C- RUB 300,000 plus 5% of the intermediary's gross income for the respective year, D- RUB 200,000 plus 5% of the intermediary's gross income for the respective year).

If the intermediary is a legal person, the accreditation fee is to be paid for each person acting in the interests of this legal person without power of attorney.

211. Regulation of the Executive Committee of FUR n 131, 18 Dec. 2008 (with further amendments).
212. Decree of the Executive Committee of FUR N 165/7, 24 Jan. 2017 with amendments http://www.rfs.ru/rfs/documents/strategies/.

These fees are to be used by the FUR only for the development of mass sport, athletes who are minors, or young sportsmen and sportswomen, for the needs of the national teams or for measures against racism, discrimination and violence in Russian football. Moreover these accreditation fees may be used for the financing of the Commission (but no more than 5% of the accreditation fees may be used). The FUR is required to publish a report concerning the use of accreditation fees annually on its official website.

Players/coaches and clubs may use the services only of the accredited intermediaries. Contracts stipulated with non-accredited individuals will be deemed to be null and void.

As in the regulations (2015), in order to prevent a conflict of interests the new regulations (Article 3(2,3)) prohibit dual representation and involvement of football officials (Article 1 of the regulations) in agency transactions.

Article 4(5) of the regulations lays down special requirements for persons intending to obtain accreditation:

For the PRO category:

- not less than five years' experience as a licensed FUR agent or as an agent at another national association, member of FIFA or;
- five years' experience as a lawyer and a higher legal degree.

For all other categories:

- not less than three years' experience as a licensed FUR agent or as an agent at another national association, member of FIFA or;
- not less than three years' experience working for an organization (subject) of professional football (club, league or FUR);
- a higher degree;
- a police record with no outstanding convictions;
- not to be a football official as specified in Article 1 of the regulations;
- absence of contractual relations with leagues, FUR, national associations, FIFA members, confederations or FIFA which may give rise to a conflict of interest;
- submission of a voluntary basic agency declaration (Forms 2 and 3 annexed to the regulations);
- payment of the accreditation fee for the category of accreditation.

The decisions concerning accreditation for the PRO category must be taken by the Commission within five working days of the presentation of the documents by the applicant. In cases in which the application for accreditation is rejected, the accreditation fee must be returned to the applicant within ten working days of the Commission's decision.

Accreditation is not required for foreign natural or legal persons whose activity is analogous to the activity of intermediaries if the contract was concluded (for a maximum period of two years) with a foreign player not registered at the time of stipulation of the contract as a Russian football player.

To receive accreditation for the categories A, B, C, D applicants must pass (Article 5 of the regulations), a special examination concerning knowledge of the legal provisions of FIFA, UEFA and FUR and be awarded a minimum points (fifteen for the category 'A', thirteen for all other categories). Two attempts are allowed. If the candidate fails at the second attempt he/she is required to wait for one year to retake the examination. The Commission is required to inform candidates about the results of the examination as well as about other decisions concerning the rejection of the application for accreditation within five working days, and return the accreditation fee within ten working days of the decision.

The intermediary is permitted to apply only for one category of accreditation. Furthermore, it is possible to change the accreditation category at any time following the same procedure established for obtaining accreditation for the desired category.

The FUR Commission on Working with Intermediaries is required to publish on the official website of the FUR (www.rfs.ru) information on all the registered agents and all the stipulated contracts. It is also required to publish all the information on remuneration of the intermediaries paid by each club in each calendar year. The Commission is required to provide within five working days of the receipt of the request the following information:

- information on the contract between the player/coach and the intermediary, or the absence of such a contract (at the written request of the club with which the player is registered);
- information on the contract between the club and the intermediary, or the absence of such a contract (at the written request of the club concerned);
- information on the contract between the player and the intermediary, or the absence of such a contract (at the written request of the player);
- information on the intermediary's contract with the club or player, or the absence of such a contract (at the written request of that intermediary).

In the case of a violation of these regulations by intermediaries, clubs or players the FUR Commission is required to publish this information on its official website (Article 8 of the regulations)

Another crucial point of the regulations concerns remuneration of the intermediary. The Regulations of 2015 (Article 6(5) established the maximum limit of 3% of the gross value of the total duration of the employment contract including amendments to the existing contract, and including various bonuses not depending on the player's or the player's team results, in line with the corresponding FIFA Regulations.

The new version of the regulations modified this limit. Pursuant to Article 12(5), the amount of remuneration is calculated on the basis of a percentage of the gross player's/coach's salary for the entire duration of the contract. Bonuses for sport results (tournament points, rankings, number of goals, time on the field) as well as non-pecuniary fringe benefits such as cars, houses, travel expenses, food, training and so on) are not included in the gross amount on which the intermediary's remuneration is calculated. What is important is that the amount of the intermediary's remuneration is determined by the parties with the exception of agents in category 'D' where the maximum amount cannot be higher than 10% of the above-mentioned gross player's income.

Neither the player nor the club is allowed to pay remuneration to an intermediary for transfers or the conclusion of employment contract for players below the age of 18 years. Players under 14 years are not permitted to stipulate contracts with an intermediary.

In the 2017 regulations the principle of maximum duration of the contact is maintained and it is limited to two years. Automatic extension is excluded but the parties are free to conclude a new contract upon expiry of the contract (Article 10(3) of the regulations).

The regulations specify in particular the obligations of the parties (Article 8 – rights and duties of the intermediary, Article 14 – duties of the players/coaches and Article 16 – duties of the clubs). Under Article 8 the intermediary should perform his/her activity on the RF territory according to the regulations on working with intermediaries, FIFA and UEFA Regulations and RF legislation. The main task of the intermediary consists promoting the interests of the represented party in finding employment, concluding contracts on the basis of a constructive dialogue and principles of legitimacy, conscientiousness and reasonableness.

Intermediaries have the right to:

- conclude contracts with players, coaches and professional football clubs in conformity with the RF legislation and FUR norms;
- apply to the CAS according to the RF laws and to adopt pretrial procedures;
- enjoy other rights according to the RF legislation and regulations on working with intermediaries.

Intermediaries are obliged to:

- represent the interests of players, coaches, clubs in good faith;
- abstain from taking part in gambling or bookmaker betting for football completions;
- observe ethical norms in sport (FUR Regulations on Ethics);
- conclude contracts only with the players older than 14 years;
- present to the Commission the document which certifies his/her annual income from intermediary activity and a copy of the fiscal declaration no later than 31 May of the following year, in the case of all intermediaries except for the category 'PRO';
- register all the contracts and their amendments with the Commission.

Intermediaries are prohibited from gambling in bookmakers' agencies and other forms of gambling. In the case of breach of this provision they may be sanctioned with a fine from RUB 10,000 to 500,000 and disqualification (withdraw of accreditation). The duration of the contract with the intermediary may not be longer than two years without the possibility of automatic renewal. The accreditation period may not be longer than five years.

Obligations of the player and coach

361. Under Article 14 the player or coach must inform the clubs about the stipulation of the contract with the intermediary and to indicate his accreditation number. The Commission may ask for information on each transaction with the intermediary and the player/coach must provide all the requested information within twenty days (unless another term is agreed in writing). In the case of failure to provide this information, the Commission has a right to apply sanctions. At the Commission's request the player/coach is obliged to inform the Commission of all the details on intermediary's remuneration as well as all the documents relating to the transaction. Any contract stipulated with the participation of an intermediary is required to contain this information.

According to Article 16 of the regulations, clubs have no right to make transfer or solidarity payments or to use the player's bonuses as part of remuneration of the intermediary. The Commission has the right to require the club to provide information on each single transaction/contract with the player/coach and the club must answer within five working days (unless another term is laid down in writing). In case of refusal, sanctions may be applied. The club with a valid contract with the accredited intermediary must engage him in bargaining if this is envisaged in the contract. All the information submitted to the FUR Commission is deemed to be confidential, except in cases specified by the regulations.

The respective sanctions for the violation of the rules established in the regulations are provided in Article 9 for intermediaries, Article 15 for players and Article 17 for clubs. The fines are specified in Annex 4 to the regulations.

For intermediaries, according to Article 9 the sanctions may include:

- warnings;
- fines of from RUB 10,000 to RUB 500,000 (Annex 4);
- suspension of accreditation (Article 7 of the regulations);
- disqualification (Article 7 of the regulations).

The sanctions may be applied jointly by the FUR Commission on Working with Intermediaries.

For the players the sanctions may include:

- warnings;
- fines of from RUB 5,000 to RUB 500.000 (Annex 4);
- disqualification for up to three months;
- disqualification for up to three months to be applied to the player only for the concluding contracts with intermediaries not accredited by the FUR or with intermediaries who violate terms for accreditation categories. Periods of non-participation in the competitions of the corresponding club for more than one month during the season or periods between the seasons are not included in the disqualification term.

The sanctions may be applied jointly by the FUR Commission on Working with Intermediaries. The sanctions on the player may be applied within two years after the

FUR Commission becomes aware (or is deemed to be aware) of the violations committed by the player.

The sanctions on the club (Article 17) may include:

- warnings;
- a prohibition on registration of new players for up to twelve months;
- fines from RUB 50,000 to RUB 1,000,000 (Annex 4).

By analogy with the sanctions applied to the player they may be applied jointly.

Unlike the previous version of the regulations, the sanctions now fall under the jurisdiction of the Commission on Working with Intermediaries and not of FUR Disciplinary Committee as before.

Suspension of accreditation and disqualification of the intermediary

362. The Commission may suspend accreditation in the following cases:

- if the intermediary fails to pay the accreditation fee (a delay of more than thirty days but no more than three months);
- in cases in which the following conditions for suspension are ascertained (as determined by the Commission):

(a) an intermediary was prosecuted for offences not related to football up to the repayment of a criminal record;

(b) there is an outstanding disciplinary sanction consisting in the ban on carrying out football-related activity (according to the decision of the FUR Disciplinary Committee) until the end of the ban.

In case of suspension of accreditation, its duration will not be increased (maximum duration of five years as specified in Article 4(2) of the regulations).

The Commission may revoke the accreditation (disqualify) the intermediary in the following cases:

- If the intermediary does not pay the accreditation fee for more than three months after the accreditation suspension.
- In the case of even one instance of flagrant violation of the regulations i.e.:

(a) forgery; or

(b) falsification of documents;

- direct or indirect influence on the match results;
- direct or indirect participation in lotteries, bookmakers agencies or totalizator regarding matches organized by FIFA, UEFA or FUR or under their aegis;
- prosecution of the intermediary for football-related activity.

The intermediary can cease his activity on a voluntary basis by filling in the claim and return the accreditation licence to the Commission. In this case the accreditation fee will not be returned. In case of disqualification the intermediary must return his accreditation licence to the Commission within seven days. The disqualified intermediary cannot be re-accredited within the next twenty-four months.

Dispute resolution

363. Under the regulations (2015) (Article 13), disputes regarding the regulations and relations with the intermediaries did not fall under the jurisdiction of the FUR and ordinary courts but had to be resolved in the national arbitration court at the Sport Arbitration Chamber whose decision was deemed to be final and could not be appealed except at the CAS in Lausanne.

Under the regulations (2017), Article 18, all the disputes must be solved in the legal bodies of the FUR (Chamber on Dispute Resolution and Committee on the Status of Players) according to the obligatory pretrial dispute resolution under the FUR Regulations on dispute resolution. Any Commission's decision concerning the denial of accreditation of the intermediary, suspension or disqualification, sporting sanctions, refusal of contract registration with the intermediary can be appealed to the FUR Appeal Committee within seven working days after the decision notification. The decision of the Appeal Committee may be subject to appeal in the CAS in Lausanne.

The regulations have four annexes. Annex 1 contains a model accreditation application by the intermediary, Annex 2 provides a model declaration for natural persons while Annex 3 provides one for legal persons. Finally, Annex 4 specifies the fines applied to clubs, intermediaries and players/coaches for breaches of the Regulations on Working with Intermediaries.

Part IV. Sport and Commerce

364. Like other countries Russia is affected by the processes of increasing professionalization, commercialization and the impact of the media on sport resulting in new challenges for the national legislator. The transition to the market economy and large-scale privatization forced national sport organizations to find ways to finance themselves. Many sources of income derive from broadcasting rights, sponsorship contracts, merchandising and use of trademark, sportsmen image and advertising. These issues are generally well regulated in the Western countries while in Russia their regulation is still at a formative stage.

§1. Intellectual Property

365. Intellectual property refers to the temporary exclusive right granted by law to the authors in relation to the results of intellectual activity as well as the non-pecuniary or moral rights of the authors to be identified as the authors of the work.

366. The legislation regulating intellectual property grants a monopoly to the authors over certain forms of use of the results of their intellectual activity, which can be used by third parties only with the permission of the authors.

367. In sport, exclusive rights regard the rights to trademarks, sport and Olympic symbols, copyright and associated rights including broadcasting of sport events and sales of tickets and lotteries. Intellectual property rights cover intangible benefits which can be transmitted from one person(s) to another. Intellectual property can be regulated in the international treaties, including bilateral and multilateral agreement. For example the treaty concluded by USSR succeeded by the RF on protection of copyright with Poland (1974), Czech Republic (1975), Austria (1981), Sweden (1986).

368. In the RF the protection of intellectual property rights is based on the norms of international treaties and Russian Constitution. Article 44 of the Constitution states that intellectual property is protected by law, while Article 71 of the Constitution refers legal regulation of the intellectual property to the competence of the Russian Federation. Current Russian legislation on the intellectual property is based on the Part IV of the Civil Code introduced by the Federal Law of 18 December 2006 N. 231-FZ. Chapter 69 covers different results of intellectual property and some special aspects. Important issue is the guarantees of personal intangible rights of sportsmen. They are reflected in Article 1228 Civil Code and Article 2 of the Labour Code – protection of personal dignity in course of labour activity.

§2. Image Rights

369. Arguably the notion of image and image rights has appeared quite recently in Russian law as in Soviet period this term was associated mainly with a critical perception of Western society.[213] Nowadays Russian legislation still lacks special norms directly regulating the image rights of people and its officially accepted legal definition. In legal literature it is possible to find some proposals in this regard. So some scholars define them as the rights acquired in course of professional activity, aimed at protection of his/her name, business reputation, integrity of private life and other intangible benefits and results of intellectual activity.[214] Usually the problem of the violation or abuse of image rights concerns famous people. In practice this problem is regulated by different norms from civil law, copyright law, antitrust law (unfair competition), etc. albeit they do not regulate image rights in a direct way.

370. Being an intangible, inalienable right of each person it is protected by a massive number of norms contained in the Russian Constitution, Civil Code and Labour Code, and federal laws from 27 July 2006 N 149-FZ 'On information, information technologies, and protection of information', from 27.07.2006 N. 152-FZ 'On personal data', from 27.12.1991 N. 2124-1 'On mass media', on 26.07.2006 N 135 –FZ 'On protection of competition'. Russian legislation on trademarks offers quite a high level of protection if registered in relation to a name of a famous person. Part of the image rights is a right to a name as reflected in the Article 150 of the Civil Code. Article 23 of the RF Constitution mentions the right of everyone to the inviolability of private life, personal and family secrets and *inter alia* to the protection of honour and good name. Article 2 of the Labour Code offers a principle of the protection of workers' dignity during working life. Article 152.1 of the Civil Code establishes important principle that the use of the image of each person is possible only upon the consent of the person. This consent may require higher levels of pay which should be reflected in employment contract.

371. In professional sport the transfer of image rights by a sportsman to a club is quite a common problem and often it happens on exclusive terms without additional remuneration by the club and express consent of the sportsmen which according to a number of Russian legal scholars contradicts Russian legislation protecting personal intangible inalienable rights.[215] This may significantly limit the rights of the sportsmen to participate in any advertisement without a written consent of the club.

372. In fact often in the employment contracts with the sportsmen the following wordings may be found:

213. E. Vostrikova, P. Poluchina, Image rights of sportsmen in Russia as institute of private law, Modern law, N 12, 2013 (in Russian). (Е. Вострикова, Р. Полухина Имиджевые права спортсменов в России как институт частного права // Современное право,N 12, 2013, ..

214. E. Vostrikova, P. Poluchina, *Image rights of sportsmen in Russia as institute of private law*, Modern Law, N 12, 2013 (in Russian). (Е. Вострикова, Р. Полухина, *Имиджевые права спортсменов в России как институт частного права* // Современное право, N 12, 2013, ..

215. Article 1265(1) Civil Code RF.

'Sportsmen grant to their clubs exclusive rights on the use of their image, name, photo and video images, graphics in advertisement of product, and services of the companies without any additional fee respect to the one established in the employment contract'. This clause is not legal as terms specified in employment contract must relate only to the labour activity. In this regard only few intangible goods can be transmitted to the employer.[216] Similar term is included also in the Annex 10 to the FUR Regulations on the Status and Transfer of Players. It states that football player agrees FUR to use his image for TV broadcasting purposes of football matches of the competitions organized by FUR and FUR has a right to pass this right to third parties without a preliminary agreement with the player or an additional compensation.[217]

373. Partially such an approach could be justified by the fact that the clubs contributed to the making-up of the image of a sportsman. However, the law should also protect sportsmen's rights by laying down an obligation on the part of the club to pay reasonable remuneration for the use of image, to request the consent and to limit the duration of these rights.

374. There are not still may court decisions in this regard. For example the image of the famous Russian boxer Nikolay Valuev was used in a video clip demonstrated in cinema before the films where he beats some noisy spectators. He claimed this in the court on the basis that it was showed without his consent and such a clip profanes his good name and is harmful for his reputation. No court decision has been taken yet. Another example is the claim of Russia skier Olympic champion Yulia Chepalova who claimed that her image was used by Adidas-Salomon (official sponsor of the Russian Skiing federation) without her consent. However normally the sportsmen do not have direct contracts with the sponsors and in her contract with the federation these rights are not regulated so her chances to win would be small and in effect she has not presented a recourse to the court.[218]

375. There is an opinion in Russian scientific literature[219] that the activity of Russian sportsmen is his/her self-expression and not a service. The services are provided by the club while a sportsman performs his work function under the employment contract so theoretically club cannot prohibit to the sportsmen to use at their discretion their name, image or pictures. However since Russian sports clubs and federations must follow the regulations of international sport federations certain limitations put on the sportsmen by the clubs in terms of the use of their image can be recognized legitimate.[220] Arguably this controversial legal institute and respective case law is still in phase of formation.

216. Alekseyev, *supra* n. 17, 717.

217. For example contracts with football club Lokomotiv contain such clauses as rights of the club to the exclusive use of sportsmen image and the right to transfer it partially or wholly to any third person without the prior consent of the player.

218. E. Vostrikova, P. Poluchina, *supra* n. 215.

219. O. A. Shevchenko, Image Rights of Sportsmen in Russia in Sport, Economics, Law and Management, M. Lawyer, N. 1, 2011 12-13. (Шевченко О. А., Имиджевые права спортсменов в России // Спорт: экономика, право, управление, М., Юрист, N. 1, 2011).

220. Shevchenko, *ibid.*

§3. Trademark

376. The trademark is regulated by the Part IV of the Civil Code. According to Article 1477(1) of the Civil Code, a trademark is the sign which serves to identify the goods of legal persons and entrepreneurs in order to distinguish them from the other products on the market. To be protected the trademark needs to be registered by the state body responsible for the intellectual property. Also international treaties contemplate the protection of trademarks.[221]

377. Legal and natural persons with the status of entrepreneur can have exclusive rights for trademark. When a trademark is registered at the state register, the owner receives the certificate. However its scope is limited to the names of products indicated in the certificate, territory of the country where it is registered and to the period of registration.

378. Under the Russian legislation a wide range of issues could be registered as a trademark including particular and exotic signs, sound, etc. (Article 1482 CC). Article 1483 CC lists the reasons for a possible refusal to register a certain trademark.

379. In Russia the term of the validity of the registration of trademark is ten years. It can be renewed for unlimited number of times for another ten years. The request must be done during the last year before the expiration term. According to Russian legislation the owner of the trademark can use the following symbol R or ® the wording 'registered trademark' to affirm the protection of his ownership right on the RF territory.

380. Another important legal principle is the obligatory use of the trademark. According to the Article 1486(1) CC, the protection of the registered trademark can be terminated if it is not used in an uninterrupted manner during any three-year period after its registration. A person concerned can present a claim to the patent litigation Chamber during these three years on condition that the trademark has not been used before this claim. This term is established in base of the Paris Convention, Article 5C(1) stating that in a country where the use of the registered trademark is obligatory, the registration can be terminated only after the expiration of the fair term and after the explanation by the person concerned of the reasons of the non-use of the trademark. Article 1486(2) states that the burden of proof lies on the trademark's owner. The right to use a trademark can be alienated to another person under the contract of alienation.

221. Paris Convention for the Protection of Industrial Property of 20 Mar. 1883 (as amended on 28 Sept. 1979) Art. 6(bis): (1) The countries of the Union undertake, ex officio if their legislation so permits, or at the request of an interested party, to refuse or to cancel the registration, and to prohibit the use, of a trademark which constitutes a reproduction, an imitation, or a translation, liable to create confusion, of a mark considered by the competent authority of the country of registration or use to be well known in that country as being already the mark of a person entitled to the benefits of this Convention and used for identical or similar goods. These provisions shall also apply when the essential part of the mark constitutes a reproduction of any such well-known mark or an imitation liable to create confusion therewith.

(2) A period of at least five years from the date of registration shall be allowed for requesting the cancellation of such a mark. The countries of the Union may provide for a period within which the prohibition of use must be requested.

(3) No time limit shall be fixed for requesting the cancellation or the prohibition of the use of marks registered or used in bad faith.

The alienation is prohibited when there is a risk to delude the consumers about the goods or/and their producer.

381. The right to use a trademark can be granted under a licensing agreement according to which one party, the owner of the exclusive right to the trademark (the licensor), grants to another party (the licensee) the right to use the trademark on certain conditions (within a certain territory or within the limits of a certain commercial venture.

382. The licensee must ensure the quality of the goods for which the trademark is used while the licensor has a right of control. Both licensor and licensee have a joint liability. The possibility to have such a kind of agreement grants to the licensor an additional possibility to advertise and diffuse the goods as well as to preserve the right for the trademark even if he does not use it during three years. Depending on the volume of the transferred rights the licences can be exclusive or non-exclusive. It is possible to conclude an agreement when a licensee can transfer the licence to third parties (sublicensing). All these kinds of agreements on exclusive use of the trademark (including the alienation agreement or licensing agreement or any other type of agreement)must be stipulated in written form and registered with a competent state federal body.

383. In sport sphere there are two types of the licence agreements: retail and for advertisement purposes. In the first case the licences are given to the clubs that can use on their production (like sport clothes, etc.) the logo or other distinctive signs of the clubs. In the second case the company buys the licence to use the logo for advertisement action.[222]

384. Among recent cases in relation to the use of trademark the one concerning Spartak may be mentioned. Public organization of physical culture and sport '(МФСО) Spartak named after Starostin' claimed to prohibit the football club Spartak to use verbal designation 'Spartak' for a series of goods like pennants, sportswear, badges, etc. So in case of positive outcome the sport club could have lost the right to produce sport attributes with its name. However the arbitration courts of four instances rejected this claim. Albeit they confirm that МФСО Spartak had the right for this trademark however they concluded a licensing agreement for non-exclusive use of this trademark with the regional public organization Football club 'Spartak-Moscow', which in turn, concluded a sublicensing agreement with the football club Spartak (which was claimed) till 2017. So no illegitimate use was discovered by the courts.[223]

§4. Merchandising

385. Merchandising is the sale of the various sport-related licensed goods with sport attributes related to the sport events and participants (clothes with the teams or players names, etc.) in the territory near to the events. In Russia merchandising is not very much spread. Pursuant to the Article 20 of the Federal Law on Sport the organizers of sport event have exclusive right for the use of the name and symbols of the sport event. The right to advertise goods and services at the place of the event belongs to

222. Alekseyev, *supra* n. 17, 2012, 722–729.
223. http://www.gazeta.ru/sport/2012/10/kz_4813685.shtml.

the event organizers. They are also entitled to the right to choose the producers of the sport equipment for such an event. Third parties can use the names of the sport events and symbols only with the written agreement of the organizers, except in cases where this information is used only for information purposes or if they acquired these rights for dissemination in the mass media.

386. According to the Article 1515(1) CC the goods where trademark or similar sign is placed illegally are considered counterfeited. Pursuant to the Article 1252(4) CC when production, diffuse, storage and transportation of the goods where the result of intellectual property is expressed and the exclusive right for the results is violated, the goods are considered to be forged and must be withdrawn from circulation and destroyed at the expenses of the violator. Under the same Article 1515(4) the owner of the trademark can ask for a compensation on his choice or (1) from RUB 5 to RUB 10 million, amount defined by the court considering the nature of the infringement; or (2) double price of the goods for which the trademark was places unlawfully or double price of the right value which is normally required for its lawful use under the comparative circumstances.

387. Pursuant to the Article 8 of the 'Olympic law', sale and another use of the products with the illegal use of the Olympic (Paralympics) symbols is considered to be unfair competition[224] with the consequences foreseen by the Russian antitrust legislation.

388. Olympic attributes such as Olympic symbol, flag, hymn, fight, torch are also protected first of all by the norms of the Olympic Charter. Any national Olympic Committee is responsible for the correct use of the Olympic symbols. NOC can use them only with the consent of the International Olympic Committee for its activity but not with the aim to generate profits.

389. Also the Law 'On advertising', Federal Law of 13 March 2006 N. 38-FZ and the Law 'On Protection of Consumers Rights' of 7 February 1992 N 2300-1 protect from unlawful use of Olympic symbols. Article 14.10 of the administrative Code establishes the types of administrative infringements and sanctions.

§5. Broadcasting Rights

390. According to the Article 20(4) of the 'Law on Sport', the organizers of the events have the exclusive right to broadcast sport events using any technologies. Third parties can use this right only upon the written consent of the organizers.

391. At the regional level, Russia is part of international agreements with CIS countries (1993)[225] which agreed that on their territory the governments must ensure

224. Federal Law of 26 Jul. 2006 N 135-FZ.

225. Commonwealth of Independent States (incudes nine countries: Armenia, Azerbaijan, Belarus, Kazakhstan, Kyrgyzstan, Moldova, Russia, Tajikistan, Uzbekistan).

the observation of the norms of Bern,[226] Genève[227] and Rome[228] conventions on the protection of copyrights and associated rights.[229]

392. In general Russian television still lacks interest to the broadcasting of sport events and thus the incomes of Russian clubs and federations are much lower than in other countries. In 2010 Russian Football Premier League earned on television broadcasting around 16 million a year compared to around 1 billion of the English Premier League. British Sky channel had around 9 million subscribers while Russian NTV plus had only 600,000 for the whole country.[230] More recent data confirm this tendency. So football club Kuban earned in the period 2013 from selling of television rights for the match of the championship and Russian Cup around 3.5 million dollars compared to Manchester United that in 2013 earned on broadcasting rights 109 million of British pounds.[231] In Russia broadcasting of many kinds of sport often happens on gratuitous basis or clubs and federations even pay for the possibility to broadcast.[232]

393. For various reasons Russian TV channels are less interested in broadcasting of sport events. This fact may be explained in part by low quality of video records, lack of entertainment and intrigue elements in Russian sport which normally make the broadcasting proposals attractive, etc. Unlike some of their international counterparts, many Russian clubs and federations do not have their own television channels or other mass media infrastructure.

Only few clubs have created them by now.[233]

§6. Advertisement

394. The Federal Law of 13 March 2006 N 38-FZ 'On advertising' defines advertising as the dissemination of information by any means and in any form with the use of any means addressed to an unlimited number of persons and aimed at attracting attention to the product or service with the purpose of their promotion on the market (Article 3 Part 1).

395. The object of the advertising can be goods, means of individualization of legal person or goods producer or seller of the goods, results of intellectual property or events (sport events, concerts, games, etc.) to which advertising is aimed (Article 3 Part 2).

396. In producing and diffusing of advertisement, the provisions of the Civil Code of RF and Federal Laws of 13 March 2006 N 38-FZ 'On advertising' and law

226. Berne Convention for the Protection of Literary and Artistic Works (1886).
227. Universal Copyright Convention (UCC), adopted in Genève, 1952.
228. Rome Convention for the Protection of Performers, Producers of Phonograms and Broadcasting Organisations (1961).
229. Alekseyev, 2012, *supra* n. 17, 745–753.
230. D. E. Nikishov, *Evolution of sport sponsorship in Russia*, Economics and Management, 8, 2010 (in Russian). (Д. Е. Никишов, *Эволюция спортивного спонсорства в России* // Экономика и управление, 8, 2010).
231. http://www.interfax.ru/sport/364794.
232. http://lenta.ru/Articles/2014/09/24/tvrights/.
233. Spartak and Rubin created their TV channels, and Zenit has its own radio station.

of 1 June 2005 N 53-FZ 'On state language of the Russian Federation' should be considered. The Law 'On Advertising' permits following methods of advertisement in sport:

- broadcasting on TV and radio in direct can be interrupted by advertisement (also by sponsored advertising) only during the breaks or stop of sport competitions and in no case should bring to the loss of substantial information on competition. Advertisement should not exceed 20% of the sport event time.

397. The law on advertising regulates also some aspects of advertisement of some kinds of products in relation to sport:

> advertisement of alcohol production including beer or drinks on its base should not contain affirmations that it has importance for social, sport or professional success or improves physical or emotional wellbeing; it should not be placed inside sport buildings or nearer than 100 meters.

398. Article 24 of the Law 'On advertising' regulates also the advertisement of medical products and medical treatments and services in the sphere of sport. It cannot be addressed to minors, should not contain personal references to concrete persons who cured diseases because of the use of advertised product/service, should not create doubts in healthy persons inducing them to use advertised products, should not affirm that safety and efficiency of the product is due to its natural origin, etc. Article 7 of the law prohibits the advertisement of drugs and psychotropic substances and their precursors as well as plants containing drug-related substances and their precursors, including doping substances.[234]

399. The advertisement of biologically active additives is regulated by the Article 25 of Law 'On advertising'. According to this article it should not:

- create impression that they are curative or have curative properties;
- refer to concrete people who allegedly improved their health;
- thanksgiving people using them;
- induce people to refuse healthy food;
- create impression about possible advantages of such additives because of the fact of trials which are obligatory for the registration of the product, or use the results of these trials to induce people to use these substances.

400. Advertisement of tobacco and tobacco-related products like pipes, kalians, etc. should not contain affirmations that it has importance for social, sport or professional success or improves physical or emotional well-being; it should not be placed inside sport buildings or nearer than 100 metres.

401. Advertisement of the artificial termination of pregnancy should contain information on potential harmful consequences of such practices for women health

234. List of prohibited doping substances adopted by WADA and confirmed by the Russian Ministry of Sport.

and should not be placed in the sites destined to the minors or youth, in the theaters, circus, libraries, sport-related places, etc. or nearer than 100 metres to them.

402. Advertisement on the betting and other hazardous games should not contain affirmations that it has importance for social, sport or professional success or improves physical or emotional well-being.

403. The recent Federal Law of 28.03.2017 N. 44–FZ ('On the amendments of some legal acts of the Russian Federation in relation to the creation of the mechanisms of increment of the incomes of young sportsmen and women and professional sportsmen and women' introduced certain amendments to the Federal Law 'On advertising' in relation to betting.

404. In particular, new clauses 2.1 and 2.2. were added to Article 27 of the law allowing exceptions to the general ban on advertising for those organizing gambling in bookmakers' agencies. It is allowed to advertise betting during broadcasting on TV and radio from 22.00 till 7.00 with the exception laid down in Article 2.1. which allows betting advertising for those organizing gambling in bookmakers' agencies at any time during live broadcasts on TV and radio or during recordings of sport competitions for 24 hours on condition that it is done only during sports broadcasting and the total duration is no longer than 20% of the maximum time allowed for advertising during sports competition broadcasting. Pursuant to Article 2.2. the organizers of gambling in bookmakers' agencies may place advertising in sports periodicals and on the internet (including sports-related websites, official websites of All Russia Sports Federations or professional sports leagues). Moreover, the individualization means of the gambling organizers in bookmaker agencies may be advertised on sports premises and on the sportsmen and women or clubs' outfits.

405. The Law 'On advertising' (Article 40) and Olympic law (Article 6) regulate advertisement during the Sochi 2014 Olympiad according to which the advertisement during the Olympiad and Paralympics inside the related objects and nearer than 1000 metres including space is possible only upon the agreement with the IOC or its entrusted entity or Paralympics Committee or its entrusted entity. The period of Olympiad is considered to be a period of one month before the event and one month after its termination (Article 2 of the 'Olympic Law'). In this period the use of the advertisement on the sport cloth and equipment used by the participants of the Olympiad or Paralympics is possible only upon the conditions foreseen by the Olympic Charter or regulations of the International Paralympics Committee. The advertisement which contains untrue statements concerning the belonging of its giver or sponsor to the Olympiad or Paralympics or false statements on its approval by the International Olympic or Paralympics Committee, Russian Olympic or Paralympics Committee, or Organization Committee of Sochi 2014 Olympiad is recognized false. Similar requirements are contained also in 'Football law' (Article 18) which admits advertisement nearer than 2000 metres from the event only upon the agreement with FIFA. During the competitions and period two days before preliminary or final sortition and day after the sortition its possible, upon the agreement with FIFA or its authorized agent to advertise beer, wine or drinks in base of wine and other good containing the name of product or producer (legal person) if they are commercial partners or contractors of FIFA and advertisement is carried out in the place of the event.

406. Among the recent court decisions in relation to the misleading and fraudulent advertisement the case concerning Russian TV channels Sport 1 and Russia 1 could be mentioned. On 26 March 2013 they broadcasted in direct a football match between Russia and Brazil from the London stadium Stamford Bridge (stadium of Chelsea). In course of broadcasting the stands of the stadium with the advertisement of the alcoholic drinks (whiskey William Lawson and vodka Huski, Zelenaya Marka and Belenkaya as well as of beer Stary Melnik and Bud) were shown. However the expertize showed that it was a computer installation and Russian FAS sanctioned ФГУП 'ВГТРК' и ZAO 'Telesport' stating that they violated Federal Law 'On advertising'. They were fined RUB 100,000 for the advertisement of beer Bud and whiskey William Lawson and RUB 150,000 for vodka Huski, Belenkaya, Zelenaya Marka and Stary Melnik.[235]

407. Sport federations may establish special provisions concerning advertisement.

For example in case of the federations of bobsleigh and skeleton where the sportsmen granted the federation the right to use their image and name in any illustrated form, in TV or any other mass media. The federation has a discretion to place the advertisement on the following parts of the sports equipment in bobsleigh:

- crash helmet (whole surface);
- competitions and training coveralls from special elastic tissue in the area of the chest, arms, back and femur;
- protective gloves;
- shoes with spikes or other special shoes;
- bobsleigh sledge.

408. In skeleton it is possible on:

- competitions and training coveralls from special elastic tissue on the front of the thigh;
- dress uniform for training and competitions given by the federation on the front of the thigh.

409. The sportsmen are prohibited to place on competition and training uniform advertisement of tobacco and alcohol drinks except wine, beer and drinks on its basis. The sportsmen are prohibited to place any advertisement during winter Olympic games.[236]

410. The Law 'On advertising'[237] contains certain facilitations for sponsored advertising. It can be integrated directly into television or radio programmes, included in religious programmes and in programmes lasting less than 15 minutes as well as it can be mentioned in social advertising. In general, sponsored advertising has major time limits with respect to the ordinary one.

235. http://pravo.ru/news/view/111300/.
236. Stukalova, *supra* n. 45 2009.
237. Article 10, 14 and 15.

§7. Sponsorship

411. Russian legislation does not provide any definition of sponsorship or sponsorship contract. The only explicit mentioning of sponsorship and sponsored advertising can be found in Article 3 of the Law 'On advertising'.[238] It defines sponsors as persons providing funds for the organization or holding of sport, cultural or any other type of events, production, television or radio broadcast or its production or use of any result of creative activity. Sponsored advertising according to this article is advertising with an obligation to name or mention the sponsor. The International Chamber of Commerce provides more complete definition of 'sponsorship' referring it to:

> any commercial agreement by which a sponsor, for the mutual benefit of the sponsor and sponsored party, contractually provides financing or other support in order to establish an association between the sponsor's image, brands or products and a sponsorship property, in return for rights to promote this association and/or for the granting of certain agreed direct or indirect benefits; ... the term 'sponsor' refers to any corporation or other legal entity providing financial or other sponsorship support;...the term 'sponsored party' refers to any individual or other legal entity owning the relevant rights in the sponsorship property and receiving direct or indirect support from a sponsor in relation to the sponsorship property.[239]

412. Although the Russian Civil Code does not provide a definition of sponsorship contracts, according to Article 8 CC RF civil rights and duties derive from agreements contemplated by law or not directly contemplated but on condition that they are not in contradiction with it.

413. According to the Article 423 CC RF regulating onerous and gratuitous types of agreements, sponsorship agreement is a commercial onerous agreement and the sponsor has a right for reciprocal services (or other kind of remuneration) from the sponsored.

414. Normally sponsorship agreement establishes the following duties of the sponsored:

- dissemination of the information on the fact and product/service of the sponsor during the period of agreement. This dissemination may be carried out in different forms like publication, press conference or other TV or radio communications;
- promotion of the sponsor's products (by participation in various events like markets or exhibitions where such a production is demonstrated;
- in case of sport goods the agreement normally specifies all possible occasions of the use of such goods including training, prize awards ceremony, press conferences, etc.

238. Federal Law from 13 Mar. 2006 N. 38-FZ 'On advertising'.

239. Advertising and marketing communication practice, Consolidated ICC Code, Building consumer trust through best practice marketing, International Chamber of Commerce, 2011, 22.

415. In the agreement it may be stated that in case of the use of the goods of another company in the occasions specified in the agreement the contract may be terminated by the sponsor unilaterally and the sanctions may be applied to the sponsored. The possibility of the use or demonstration of the goods of other companies may be separately agreed in the sponsorship agreement. The agreement may include clauses on the prohibition to sell or transfer of the sponsor's goods to the third parties. This relates to a series of services which may be provided to the sponsor like free room during the events, free tickets, right to use the names of the sportsmen, etc. In case of the sponsorship of the clubs (federations, teams, etc.) the sponsor may also require the right to use names, photo and images of the sportsmen for the advertisement purposes as well as accountability regarding the use of the sponsor's finding. The sponsor may also require his trademarks being visible during the use or demonstration of his products. The other sponsor's rights may include the right to acquire from third parties the goods or other products transferred then to the sponsored, the right to involve third parties in supply of the goods, the right to produce copies of the (sport) goods using the trademarks of the sponsored with the right to sell them (on this occasion a royalty condition may be included), etc.

416. Also the sponsored have the rights which may be reflected in the sponsorship agreement. During the validity of the sponsorship agreement they may conclude contracts with other sponsors if it is not otherwise agreed. They can also approve the design to be used on the sponsor's products, their quantity, assortment and delivery terms. The sponsor is under the obligation to pay sponsorship fee on terms agreed by the parties. Special fee may be established for the important events like Olympiads, etc. Moreover bonuses for outstanding sport results (records, medals) may be contemplated as well as scholarships or bonuses to the outstanding sportsmen and coaches. The parties may include other terms like modality of tax and duties payment, possibilities of audit or other types of control, use of intermediary, etc. Also the conditions of termination may be specified.[240]

417. Sports-related sponsorship may be of different kinds.

Sponsorship of ready from the organizational point of view, competitions, both at the international and national level. In this case the advantage for the sponsor is availability of a wide choice of different sponsorship packages. The disadvantage is a contemporary presence of other sponsors. However in such cases they may divide the spheres of activities.

418. Creation of the own sport event for a concrete brand or organization and its promotion. It is more difficult for practical realization but can offer major profits.

419. During Sochi 2014 Olympic games the issue of sponsorship was reflected in the 'Olympic law'. So Article 8 of this Law introduces the norms of fair competition and intends under sponsors foreign and Russian organizations which concluded sponsorship agreement with the Sochi Olympic games Organizing Committee, International Olympic or Paralympic Committees. The misleading or false information about the own involvement as a sponsor in the games is considered to be unfair completion and such is sanctioned under the Russian antitrust legislation. Article 6(3)

240. S. V. Alekseyev, *Legal regulation of sponsorship* in Sport: Economics, Law and Management, N. 4, 2011 (in Russian). (С. В. Алексеев, *Правовое регулирование спортивного спонсорства* // Спорт: экономика, право, управление, N. 4, 2011).

of the 'Olympic law' defines the modality of advertising activity during the period of the games and states that any advertisement containing misleading information on the involvement of the advertiser including sponsors, to the Olympic or Paralympic games or about the presumed approval of his candidature by the International or Russian Olympic or Paralympic or Sochi 2014 Organizing Committee is considered unfair.

420. Unlike charity makers who act basing on the principles of voluntariness and disinterestedness[241] sponsors expect some profits from their sponsored clients. However it should be taken into account that sponsorship may be onerous and gratuitous. In a situation when a sponsor does not require to be officially mentioned as a sponsor but asks that information on his goods and services appear during the sponsored events, it is not considered a charity but an advertisement.[242]

421. Sponsorship advertisement under the Law 'On advertising' has a number of advantages with respect to the ordinary advertisement.

422. In general sponsorship market in Russia is very sensitive to certain legal changes. So after the ban of alcohol production advertisement (Article 21 of the Law 'On advertising') on TV and radio and restriction of the advertisement of beer a number of Russian and foreign sponsors[243] left the market of sport sponsoring. Another negative point for attraction of sponsors is low quality of the stadiums, low level of attendance of the stadiums, low level of the internal to the stadiums infrastructures and entertainment during the breaks, small number of café, restaurants and shops, absence of car parking, low level of safety. There are a few new stadiums and often clubs lack funds for the modernization of the existing ones. Such a diffused phenomenon as naming (attribution of a name of a sponsor to a sport infrastructure) widely used abroad is still underdeveloped in Russia.[244]

423. In general Russian sport industry still lags behind foreign one in terms of entertainment and intrigue. There are still very few, respect to other countries, specialized in sponsorship agencies able to provide complete and transparent information on the sport market and bring together potential sponsors and sponsored. For these and other reasons the professional approach to a sport sponsorship in Russia is often lacking and it is performed either on an amateur basis due to the passion for sport of single sponsors or it is dictated by short-term economic interests.

424. Finally the lack of the legal regulation may represent an obstacle to the effective development of sponsorship in Russia. As a result the sport of youth and some less popular kinds of sport lack the attention of serious sponsors. Also in small cities sponsorship is often problematic. Major legal regulation by means of a special law on sponsorship as well as additional fiscal benefits to the sport sponsors could undoubtedly simulate the development of this institute in Russia.

241. Federal Law from 11 Aug. 1995 N. 135-FZ 'On charitable activity and charity organisations'.
242. Alekseyev, 2012, *supra* n. 17, 699–710.
243. Baltica, Efes, Parliament, Nemiroff.
244. D. E. Nikishov, *supra* n. 231.

Part V. Social Security

425. Considering significant physical overload and high injury rate sometimes resulting in partial or permanent invalidity, professional sport requires particular attention to be paid to the insurance issues. In comparison with the level of social protection and insurance legislation of professional sportsmen and coaches existing in many Western countries, in Russia general level is still quite modest even if the government is currently working on the set of measures to raise social protection of this category of workers. The strategy of the development of the state policy in the sphere of physical culture and sport in the RF up to 2020[245] (Chapter VIII, Article 18) intends to strengthen the measures[246] of social protection of sportsmen and coaches including targeted social assistance for outstanding Russian sportsmen. These measures include *inter alia*:

- special measures including high-level medical treatment;
- facilitations in admission to high-level state and municipal educational institutions;
- benefits and preferences in pension law including additional pension support.

426. The Law on Sport does not contain any specific provisions in this regard so players like other categories of workers are covered by the general legislation on obligatory medical insurance (Federal Law from 29 November 2010 N. 326-FZ 'On obligatory medical insurance in the RF'), insurance in case of temporary disability to work (Federal Law from 29 December 2006 N. 255-FZ 'On obligatory social insurance in case of temporary disability to work and maternity leave'). Moreover in case of disability the sportsmen are also covered by the provisions of the law from 24 November 1995 N. 181-FZ 'On social protection of disable in the RF', insurance indemnity in case of professional diseases and injuries (Federal Law from 24 July 1998 N 125-FZ 'On obligatory social insurance against incidents at work and professional diseases') and insurance and pensions (Federal Law from 15 December 2001 N. 167-FZ 'On obligatory pensions insurance in the RF').

427. Labour Code contains some new provisions in this regard. In particular Article 348(2) LC lays down employers' obligation to take out life and medical insurance for sportsmen. Moreover, additional medical insurance coverage is required which amount is however left at the discretion of employers or sport federations.

In football the Regulations on the Status and Transfer of Players require clubs:

245. Approved by the governmental order from 7 Aug. 2009 N 1101p.

246. Some specific measures on social protection of sportsmen and coaches were included in the law from 29 Apr. 1999 N. 80-FZ (on Physical Culture and Sport in RF) but then were 'lost in transition'.

- to provide obligatory social insurance for players pursuant to the labour legislation or other normative acts of the RF;
- to cover the cost of health and safety insurance as well as medical insurance in order to enable players to receive medical services in addition to those required by law and to specify their terms;
- to organize at their own expense compulsory preliminary and annual periodical medical check-ups for the player, extra medical check-ups at the request of players and medical advice;
- to make available financial assistance in the case of a temporary inability to work due to sports-related injury under the employment contract, in order to bring the temporary disability benefit in line with the average monthly salary of players if such a benefit is lower and income support is not provided by supplementary insurance schemes

Moreover, the amended version of the Regulations on the Status and Transfer of Players (effective from 1 January 2016) introduced into Article 7 a new clause 7^1 laying down for football clubs an obligation in cases in which a player suffers a sports-related injury during a sports event in the course of the validity of the employment contract. In such cases the club is required to cover the following expenses not covered by medical insurance and obligatory medical insurance, with the consent of the club's medical officer (unless otherwise agreed by the parties in the contract):

- expenses in relation to the medical treatment of the player on the RF territory and abroad (if stipulated in the contract), including related travel expenses;
- expenses in relation to the purchase of necessary medical products and individual care;
- expenses covering special external medical care.

428. Generally speaking there are two elements in the insurance system:

(1) compulsory insurance (common for all citizens regardless of occupation);
(2) voluntary insurance.

429. Compulsory insurance is governed by the Federal Law of 28 July 1998, N 125-FZ 'On the compulsory insurance against accidents at work and occupational diseases'. However, in the case of professional players the cost of medical treatment may be too high to be covered by the compulsory insurance and supplementary (voluntary) insurance is needed.

430. Federal Law from 5 April 2013 N 36-FZ amending Article 9 of the law from 24.07.1998 N 125-FZ 'On obligatory social insurance against incidents at work and professional diseases' and Article 1(2) of the Federal Law from 29.12.2006 N

255-FZ 'On obligatory social insurance in case of temporary inability to work and maternity leave' introduced the upper limits on the amount of the indemnity.[247]

431. This amount consists of 100% of the employee's wage and does not depend on seniority but it cannot be lower than the monthly minimum wage. However from 2013 the upper limit is established. Pursuant to the new rules its amount cannot be higher than four monthly insurance contributions.[248] Such an amount is adjusted on yearly base. For 2015, considering that maximum threshold of monthly security contribution is RUB 65,330.00 per month, the maximum amount of indemnity would be RUB 261,320.00 per month (RUB 65,330.00 × 4). In some cases it can be lowered by law[249] on the following reasons:

- violation of the regime prescribed by the medical officer;
- omission to undergo periodical medical check-ups;
- injury caused by use of alcohol, drug or other kind of intoxication.

432. In these circumstances the amount cannot be higher than 1 MROT[250] (RUB 5,965 for 2015)[251] per month. In the regions where the additional coefficient to a MROT is foreseen the amount must be multiplied by this coefficient.

433. Already the first analysis shows that these new legislative provisions cannot be fully acceptable for the professional sportsmen whose average wages are much higher as well as the level of risk. These latter circumstances were in particular taken into consideration by the legislator. According to the 'classification of the kinds of economic activity according to a kind of risk' adopted by the circular of the Ministry of Labour 25.12.2012 N 625-н the activity of professional sportsmen for some unknown reasons is recognized as non-risk related and refereed to a class 1 of professional risks category (the lowers from thirty-two specified in the above-mentioned classification) so the minimum contributions are established in this regard. In this relation some scandalous facts happened in 2012 when the players of Zenit, St. Petersburg received from the state huge indemnities relating to professional injuries. In 2011, 53% of the expenses of the St. Petersburg Social Security Fund paid to twelve Zenit players with the total amount of RUB 162 million while Zenit, on its part, paid to the Social Fund only RUB 6.2 million of contributions.

434. In light of the high traumatism of sport often requiring long and expensive cures and rehabilitation (the amounts of such treatments are generally much higher than the thresholds established by the obligatory insurance schemes) and considering that there are many young sportsmen under 14–18 years, a large number of problems should be resolved in base of the additional voluntary insurance. Russian practice of

247. In any such a limitation seems to be in contradiction with the constitutional court opinion which in the decision from 22 Mar. 2007 N 4-П recognized the establishing of upper limits of the indemnity related to the maternity leave is unfair as worsens he position of workers whose wages are higher.
248. Article 9(2) of Federal Law from 24 Jul. 1998 No. 125-FZ.
249. Article 1(2), Art. 8 (1(2)) of the Federal Law from 29 Dec. 2006 No. 255-FZ.
250. MROT – minimum official monthly wage which is annually adjusted, *See* fn. 32.
251. Article 1 of the Federal Law from 01 Dec. 2014 N 408-FZ.

obligatory social insurance have its peculiarities.[252] So voluntary insurance covers sportsmen in the following cases:

- during sportsmen competition periods abroad according to the general rules established by sport federations of competition organizers;
- during periods of training on the RF territory;
- in case of insurance of the members of national teams the insurance does not cover the whole calendar year but only the period when sportsmen are staying in the national teams, including periods abroad;
- the insurance from professional injuries and diseases is carried out in a form of collective insurance when the insurers are sport, clubs, federations or other sport organization.

435. The insurance against incidents normally grant to the sportsmen four basic guarantees:

(1) guarantee in case of death (the establish amount established in the insurance policy is paid);
(2) guarantee in case of disability (60%–90% of the amount laid down in the insurance policy is paid depending of the degree of disability and terms of agreement);
(3) guarantees in case of temporary disability (payment of daily indemnity for the period of medical treatment and rehabilitation). This guarantee is limited in time which is established in the insurance agreement from 30 to 365 days or forfeit payment from 5% to 100% of the insurance amount depending on the degree and consequences of disability;
(4) guarantees of medical treatment coverage (hospitalization, outpatient treatment, medicines and care).

436. In cases of national teams the insurer is the centre of sport training of the national teams (ZSP) within the jurisdiction of the Ministry of Sport.

437. As for additional safeguards for professional players the presidential decree introduced a special monthly allowance for certain categories of sportsmen such as members of national Olympic teams,[253] sportsmen and women taking part in the Paralympics and the Deaf Sports movements.[254] According to the Federal Law of 22 August 1996 N. 125-FZ 'On higher professional education', prizewinners and champions of the Olympics, Paralympics and Deaf Olympics can be admitted to the higher education institutions with the purpose to acquire sport-related qualifications without entrance exams.

252. S. V. Alekseyev, *Legal aspects of personal insurance in sport*, in Sport, Economy, Law and Management) (in Russian). (С. В. Алексеев, *Правовые аспекты личного страхования в спорте* // Спорт: экономика, право, управление', N 2, 2014).
253. The Decree of the President of the RF of 6 Jul. 2002 N. 692.
254. The Decree of the President of the RF of 6 Dec. 2003 N. 1423. *See also* the Decree of the President of the RF of 31 Mar. 2011 N. 368 regarding allowances for certain categories of sportsmen and women.

438. The federal subjects of the Russian Federation can enact special legislation to ensure additional income support for outstanding sportsmen, and there are also special charity funds for champions. A number of subjects of the RF have already adopted such laws (Moscow, St. Petersburg (and their areas (oblast[255]), oblast' of Perm, Omsk, Tyumen, Bashkortostan, Buryatia, Altay, etc. Moreover in 2005 a special fund in support of Olympic winners was created. Russian Union of sportsmen which unifies almost all Olympic champions and prizewinners is active in the field of charity and general support of top-level sportsmen.[256]

439. Pensions: Actually sportsmen are entitled to the general pension conditions under the pension legislation.

440. Among the relevant pension legislation the following acts should be mentioned: law from 16 July 1999 N. 165-FZ 'On the foundations of compulsory social insurance', Federal Law from 15 December 2001 N. 167-FZ 'On compulsory pension insurance in the RF', Federal Law from 17 December 2001 N. 173 'On labour pensions', Federal Law from 24 July 2009 N. 212-FZ 'On insurance contributions in the Pension Fund, Social Fund, Federal fund of compulsory medical insurance of the RF', Federal Law from 28 December 2013 N. 400-FZ 'On insurance pensions'.

441. Among few particular measures in relation to professional sportsmen one in particular may be mentioned. So under the Law of 12 February 1993 N. 4468-I, the champions of Olympics, Paralympics and Deaf Olympics have the right to a 50% allowance in relation to disability pensions, superannuation pensions and survivors' pensions.

442. The official pension age in Russia is 60 years for men and 55 – for women.[257] Recently some proposals to change general pension rules for the sportsmen were put forward. Main idea is to permit outstanding sportsmen categories (champions and prizewinners of Olympic games, Paralympics, Deaf Olympics, world champions and Europe champions) earlier retirement. Similar provisions could be adopted also in relation to the coaches. If such a law will be adopted the sportsmen would be able to retire at any age after twenty-five years of service.

443. Albeit undoubted progress in elaboration of specific measures aimed at social protection of the professional sportsmen in Russia, there are still evident inconsistencies of the existing legislation which remains fragmentary and targets mainly some narrow categories of sportsmen such as top-level sportsmen and champions while leaving broader categories of sportsmen and coaches without adequate social protection.[258] In this relation improvement is expected in the field of compulsory and voluntary insurance where the minimum terms and standards for employers should be established. Major guarantees in relation to the medical support of the sportsmen leaving top-level sport should be contemplated. The retirement age reduction is an

255. Regional unit of federal territorial division of Russia (equivalent of area).
256.), (O. A. Brusnikina, S. V. Alekseyev, Problems of social protection of sportsmen in the RF, legal solutions in Sport, Economy, Law and Management, , N. 3, 2011 (in Russian). (О. А. Брусникина, С. В. Алексеев, Проблемы социальной защиты спортсменов в Российской Федерации: *законодательные пути решения* // Спорт, Экономика, Право, Управление, N. 3, 2011).).
257. Article 7 Federal Law 173-FZ from 17 Dec. 2001.
258. Alekseyev, *supra* n. 17, 2012, 377–390.

important measure that could provide additional financial guarantees to the sportsmen as well as to provide them an important opportunity to adapt to a new profession, if they wish so, after the termination of the sport carreer. In general a complex of measures is necessary to provide adequate social protection to all the categories of sportsmen, mass and elite sport included, and create for them most favourable conditions for practising sport.

Part VI. Collective Bargaining in Sport

444. Trade unions in the RF are regulated by law from 12.01.1996 N. 10-FZ 'On professional unions, their rights and guarantees'. In relation to the sport, the 'Law on Sport' (Article 5(11)) lists them among the subjects of Physical Culture in Russia. They are aimed to represent the interests of sportsmen, coaches and other stakeholders. In Russia the main trade union in the field of sport is Profsporttur.[259] It was founded on 11 December 1991. This trade union is a part of Russian trade union movement and acts accordingly to the Constitution of the RF and other laws. Profsporttour is a volunteer non-commercial public trade union organization acting on the whole territory of RF and having the status of the All-Russian organization.

445. Among its main tasks are the following:

- protection of the rights and interests of the members in case of individual labour disputes;
- elaboration of measures to raise the life standards of its members;
- participation in social and economic policy, drafting of laws and other legal acts concerning social and labour questions for the workers in the sphere of physical culture, sport and tourism including professional sportsmen and veterans of sport;
- representation of workers' interests in social partnership and carrying out collective bargaining as well as the control over the performance;
- taking part in elaboration and discussion together with state bodies and other interested organizations of socio-economic programmes to guarantee protection of trade union members rights and promotion of physical culture, sport and tourism;
- participation in advancement of the proposals aimed to improve social, medical and pension rights of the workers in the sphere of sport and tourism;
- taking part in drafting state and regional programmes of employment and promoting measures to provide social protection for workers dismissed because of liquidation or reorganization of enterprises or collective redundancies and carrying out of control over employment legislation observance;
- participation in the settlement of collective labour disputes (including strikes);
- participation and organization of collective trade union actions such as meetings, demonstrations, picketing, etc;
- participation in the election of bodies of state power and local self-administration, referendums, according to federal laws and laws of the subjects of the RF;
- control over the compliance by the employers of the labour law and local normative acts (containing norms in matter of health and safety), fulfilment of collective agreements and contracts;

259. http://www.profsporttur.ru/.

- participation in practical implementation of the main directions of state policy in matter of labour protection and where necessary, creation of the TU inspections;
- participation in the expertise of health and safety at the workplace in the sites under construction or already constructed as well as of the relative equipment;
- control over the observance of norms of health and safety during sport training and sport events;
- participation in control over the observance of laws during privatization of state and municipal property, including the social one and representing workers interests in the respective commissions;
- supply to the TU members necessary information and other legal, organizational or material assistance, etc;
- creation of the legal services and consultations for protection of social and labour rights of the TU members and representation of their interest in the courts;
- participation in the promotion of youth, gender and other programmes;
- participation in the management of state funds of some kinds of obligatory social insurance and other social funds and control over their use;
- organization of the cultural mass sport and health events for TU members and their families;
- performance of other activities related to the TU aims not prohibited by the Russian legislation.

446. Besides sectoral TU there are also special TU in some kinds of sport. In 2005 some leading football players[260] created interregional public organization 'Trade union of football players and coaches of Russia' (ПСФТ)[261] aimed at protection of interests of sportsmen and coaches. It is recognized by the FIFPRO. This TU represents players' interests, helps in solving conflicts with the clubs, provides assistance in search of new teams, consultations (legal and financial and other), medical assistance and assistance in case of conflicts with the agents.

447. Among its main initiatives the following can be mentioned:

- requirement to take into consideration regional climatic peculiarities existing in the RF in different seasons during drafting of the competitions calendar for a sport season;
- to ensure players regular wage payments by leagues and clubs. For this purpose it is proposed to deny the licence to the clubs which do not have sufficient financial actives to be used in case of their bankruptcy;
- to permit in any moment to register for competitions the players, members of the schools representing structural divisions of clubs, or players who became unemployed because of injury or club exclusion from the competitions;
- to ensure the observance of labour legislation in matter of insurance of sportsmen and not register labour contracts between clubs and players without adequate insurance policy;
- to eliminate compensation after the expiry of labour contracts for sportsmen below the age of 23;

260. Such as Andrey Arshavin, Alexandr Ryazanzev, Roman Pavluchenko, etc.
261. http://www.psft.ru/.

- to include players and coaches representatives in the Executive Committee of FUR and in Dispute Resolution Chamber.

448. Another trade union in football is All-Russian trade union of football players (ОПСФ)[262] which was established at the institutional conference of 4 September 2010.[263] It is recognized by the FUR. The main tasks of this TU according to its articles of association are:

- representation and protection of rights and interests of players in case of individual and collective disputes;
- representation of collective and individual interests in relations with FUR, clubs and leagues, participation in state programmes of employment;
- preparation of measures aimed at social protection of football players, social and medical insurance and medical provisions;
- participation in elaboration of norms of sport regulations relating to competitions;
- control over the law observance, participation in dispute settlement, etc.[264]

449. Also in hockey there is a Kontinental Hockey League Players' Trade Union (KHLPT).[265]

450. According to the Article 2.8.2. of the collective agreement for professional hockey players for 2008–2009 it carries out following activity:

- unifies and coordinates the activity of the primary trade union organizations (or other kinds of trade union organizations) in base of the Statute for the protection of the economic, social, labour and professional rights and interests of its members;
- performs collective bargaining with the aim of drafting, conclusion or modification of the agreement with the employer and controls over its performance;
- represents and defends the interests of the trade union members, primary trade unions (or other trade union organizations) in the league, state, municipal and judicial bodies;
- forms and adopts requirements towards hockey clubs, employers' associations, league, state and municipal bodies and adopts decisions about strikes or other collective actions;
- contacts federal legislative and executive bodies with proposals to adopt legal or other normative acts regarding the protection of the interests of hockey player as sportsmen;
- controls over clubs observance of labour legislation and other normative acts in the field of labour law;
- performs an independent expertize of employment conditions;
- participates in the investigation of the work-related accidents and professional diseases;

262. http://footballunion.ru/.
263. Whose leader is Vagis Hidiatullin (former player of Moscow Spartak).
264. http://sportwiki.to.
265. http://www.khlptu.ru/.

- collects information from the clubs about number of players, their wages and wages indebtedness and redundancy measures;
- stimulates its members to respect their duties and rules of internal discipline and health and safety.

451. In 2015 a sectoral collective agreement was concluded covering the organizations under the jurisdiction of the Ministry of Sport between the Ministry of Sport and Profsporttur covering sportsmen, players and other employees in the field of sport and physical culture for the period of 2015–2017.

452. The agreement regulates employment relationship of sportsmen and coaches, in particular working time, wages, vocational training and retraining, attestation, guarantees of health and safety at the workplace, additional guarantees and compensations, protection of the employment and social rights of the youth, pensions and social guarantees of the workers, measures to foster employment, guarantees to trade union officials and finally, rights and duties of the signatory parties. This agreement reproduces in part already existing provisions of the Labour Code, the Law on Sport and laws on trade unions and many of its clauses are of a generic and declaratory nature and need further concretization in the other normative acts like more specific collective agreements for a determinate kind of sport, internal sports federations regulations or individual employment contracts.

453. In general in the sphere of professional sport for a number of reasons trade union movement is not widely spread. In many kinds of sport trade unions are absent. This can be explained by the peculiarity of the sport industry as the regulations where the main employment conditions, including the determination of the salaries of single are set forth, are adopted by the international and All-Russian sport federations without real participation of trade unions. Moreover their participation in the internal dispute resolution bodies of the federations is often ignored.[266] Considering general complexity to organize official strike in Russia, in sport sphere it is even more complicated considering low trade union presence in the sector and lack of solidarity among workers employed in sport sphere where not the last role plays great disparity of employment conditions and remuneration levels not only in relation to different kinds of sport but also within the same teams as well. For this reason the foreign experience could provide some useful insights for the improvement of the social dialogue in sport in Russia.

266. Shevchenko, *supra* n. 221, 2014, 59.

Conclusion

454. Arguably Russian sports law is still at a formative stage even if many tendencies in the international sports development linked to its increasing professionalization, commercialization and 'medialisation' have been already, albeit with different success, implemented in Russia. It is an inevitable process induced by globalization affecting any country wishing to be active at the international sport arena. Considering pyramidal structure of sport organization and the fact that national sport federations are part of the international sport federations and need to comply with their rules it is possible to speak about a transnational sport regulation coexisting with the national one. In order to make this coexistence as 'peaceful' as possible and to ensure maximum legal protection to all the sport stakeholders, it is necessary to align national legal norms with the international ones. In fact many legal measures implemented in Russia in recent decades were aimed to reach this goal.

455. Albeit the significant role of the state in the regulation of sport, some priorities and spheres of intervention have changed respect to the past. Nowadays many aspects are delegated to the autonomy of the subjects of the Russian Federation and national sport federations in such matters as adoption of their internal regulations in conformity with the standards laid down by the corresponding international federations. Moreover they are granted major discretion in a number of economic and entrepreneurial issues. More attention is paid to the legal regulation of such aspects as employment relations in sport, possibilities to attract foreign players, coaches and other sport personnel, security of sport events and spectators behaviour, promotion of sport justice at various levels in order to raise effectiveness of dispute resolution. Respect to this latter issue, alternative forms of dispute resolution are gaining increasing popularity. In line with the world trends in sport industry, commercial aspects of sport such as protection of intellectual property, image rights, broadcasting and other mass media rights, merchandising, sponsorship continue to evolve and gain legal recognition at national level. Logically the progress affected different spheres to a different extent. Some aspects, mainly relating to doping, the immigration law, social protection of sportsmen including pension rights and guarantees in case of professional injuries or disability need further attention even if general policy directions in this regard have been already outlined. Finally social dialogue and collective bargaining in sport are expected to have stronger role in future and from this point of view of international experience, especially of the countries with consolidated traditions of social dialogue, may provide for Russia a sort of inspiration.

456. In general apparently sport law is increasingly gaining its autonomy on the juridical arena as an independent branch of law and even if the process is slow, the possibility to have one day a Russian 'lex sportiva' is not seen today as 'utopia'. Albeit the intensiveness of the international pressures and receptivity of international regulatory experience in many legal and non-legal spheres, Russia remains a country which historically may be proud of its outstanding sporting traditions and distinguished sportsmen. From this point of view it preserves its own legal, cultural and other traditions and where necessary often revives positive experience of the past somehow lost in transition to the market economy.

Selected Bibliography

Alekseyev S. V., *Sports law in Russia. Employment relations in sport*, Unity Dana, Law and legislation, Moscow, 2014 (in Russian). (Алексеев С. В., *Спортивное право России. Трудовые отношения в спорте.* Юнити Дана, Закон и право, М. 2014).

Alekseyev S. V., *Legal aspects of personal insurance in sport*, in Sport, economics, law and management) (in Russian). (С. В. Алексеев, *Правовые аспекты личного страхования в спорте* //Спорт: экономика, право, управление, N 2, 2014).

Alekseyev S. V., *Sports law in Russia*, Unity Dana, Law and legislation, 3rd edition, Moscow, 2012 (in Russian). (Алексеев С. В., *Спортивное право России*, Юнити Дана, Закон и право, 3 издание, М. 2012).

Alekseyev S. V., *Legal regulation of sport sponsorship in Sport*: economics, law and management, N. 4, 2011 (in Russian). (Алексеев С. В., *Правовое регулирование спортивного спонсорства* // Спорт: экономика, право, управление, N. 4, 2011).

Alekseyev S. V., *International sports law*, Unity Dana, Law and Legislation, Moscow, 2008 (in Russian). (Алексеев С. В., *Международное спортивное право*, Юнити Дана, Закон и право, М. 2008).

Alekseyev S. V., *Sports law in Russia*, Unity Dana, Law and Legislation, Moscow, 2005 (in Russian). (Алексеев С. В., *Спортивное право России*, Юнити Дана, Закон и право, М. 2005).

Babaev R. Y., *The peculiarities of the legal regulation of labour of foreign citizens in the sphere of physical culture and sport in the RF*, Moscow, Dissertation, 2014 (in Russian). (Р. Ю. Бабаев. *Особенности правового регулирования труда иностранных граждан в сфере физической культуры и спорта в Российской Федерации*, Диссертация, М. 2014).

Borisov A. N., *Commentary* to the Federal Law "On Physical culture and sport in Russian Federation", Justizinform, 2009 (in Russian) *(Борисов А.Н., Комментарий* к Федеральному закону "О физической культуре и спорте в Российской Федерации" (постатейный), Юстицинформ, 2009).

Brilliantova A. M., *Sport arbitration as means of regulation of sport related disputes (comparative legal aspects)*in Theory and practice of physical culture, 6, 2004 (in Russian). (Бриллиантова А. М., *Спортивный арбитраж как способ рассмотрения споров в области спорта (сравнительно-правовой аспект)* // Теория и практика физической культуры, 6, 2004.

Selected Bibliography

Brusnikina, O. A., Alekseyev S. V., *Problems of social protection of sportsmen in the RF, Legal solutions* in Sport: economy, law and management) (in Russian). (О. А. Брусникина, С. В. Алексеев, *Проблемы социальной защиты спортсменов в Российской Федерации: законодательные пути решения* // Спорт: экономика, право, управление, N. 3, 2011).

Erofeev A.V., *Peculiarities of Tort Liability in Sport*, in Vestnik of Volgograd University, 3(20), 2013 (in Russian) (Ерофеев А. В., *Об особенностях деликтной ответственности в области спорта* // Вестник Волгоградского Государственного Университета, Юриспруд. N. 3 (20), 2013.

Gusov K. N., *Activity of the Dispute Resolution Chamber of the Football Union Russia*, materials of the 5th international conference *on Sports Law: Prospects for Development*, Moscow, 2011 (in Russian). (Гусов К. Н., *Деятельность палаты по разрешению споров российского футбольного союза*, материалы V международной научно-практической конференции *Спортивное право: перспективы развития* М., 2011).

Gusov K. N., Scevchenko O. A., *Sports law*, Moscow, 2009 (in Russian) (Гусов К. Н., Шевченко О. А., *Спортивное право*), М. 2009.

Hendrickx F., *The Simutenkov Case: Russian players are equal to European Union players*, The International Sports Law Journal, N. 3 2005.

Kirilyuk O., *Lex* sportiva – *the concept of transnational sports law*, in Law and life, 8/3, 2013 (in Russian). (О. Кирилюк, *Lex sportiva – концепция транснационального спортивного права* // Закон и жизнь, N. 8(3), 2013).

Korshunova T. Y., *The development of legislation on labour of professional sportsmen*, in Labour Law, N. 5, 2006 (in Russian). (Коршунова Т. Ю., *Развитие законодательства о труде профессиональных спортсменов* // Трудовое право, N 5, 2006).

Nikishov D. E., *Evolution of sport sponsorship in Russia*, in Economics and management, 8, 2010 (in Russian). (Никишов Д. Е., *Эволюция спортивного спонсорства в России* // Экономика и управление, N. 8, 2010).

O'Mahony M., *Sport in the USSR. Physical culture- visual culture*, Reaktion books, London, 2006 (In Russian). (М. О'Махоуни, *Спорт в СССР, Физическая культура – визуальная культура*, Новое литературное обозрение, перевод с английского Е. Ляминой, А. Фишман, М, 2010).

Pogosyan, E. V., *Forms of resolution of sports disputes.* Monograph, Wolters Kluwer, 2011 (in Russian). (Погосян Е. В., *Формы разрешения спортивных споров*. Монография, Волтерс Клувер, 2011).

Ponkin I. V., Soloviev A. A, Ponkina F. I., *Legal protection against illegal behaviour of sport fans,* Moscow, 2014 (in Russian). (Понкин И. В., Соловьев А. А., Понкина А. И., *Правовое обеспечение противодействия противоправному поведению спортивных болельщиков*, М., 2014).

Selected Bibliography

Prokopets M., *Limits on foreign professional players competing in the Russian Federation: problems and prospects* in The International Sports Law Journal, N. 3–4, 2009.

Prokopets M., Rogachev D., De Veger F., *Sport disputes resolution*, Moscow, Statute, 2012 (in Russian). (М. Прокопец, Д. Рогачев, Ф. Де Вегер, *Разрешение футбольных споров*, М. Статут, 2012).

Rymkevich O. P. and Grammatikov N., *The regulation of employment contracts for professional football players: the case of Russia*, in European Sports Law and Policy Bulletin, I-2011.

Saraev V. V., *Criminal law protection of contemporary professional sport in Russia*. Dissertation, Omsk, 2009 (in Russian). (Сараев В. В. *Уголовно-правовая охрана современного профессионального спорта в России*, Диссертация, Омск, 2009).

Shevchenko O. A., *Legal doctrine of labour regulation in professional sport and its realization in Russia*. Dissertation, Moscow, 2014 (in Russian). (Шевченко О. А, *Правовая доктрина регулирования труда в сфере профессионального спорта и пути ее реализации в России*. Диссертация, М., 2014).

Shevchenko O. A., *Image rights of sportsmen in Russia* in Sport: economics, law and management, M. Lawyer, N. 1, 2011. (Шевченко О. А., *Имиджевые права спортсменов в России*// Спорт: экономика, право, управление, М., Юрист, N. 1, 2011).

Soloviev A. A., *The concept of the Sport Code in the Russian Federation*, Moscow, 2009 (in Russian). (Соловьёв А. А., *Концепция проекта Спортивного кодекса Российской Федерации*, 2009).

Stukalova Y. V., *Commentary* to the Chapter 54.1 of the Russian Labour Code "Peculiarities of the regulation of labour of sportsmen and coaches", Garant system, 2009. (Стукалова, Ю. В. *Комментарий* к главе 54.1 Трудового кодекса Российской Федерации "Особенности регулирования труда спортсменов и тренеров" (постатейный), Система Гарант, 2009).

Vostrikova E. A., Poluchina P. E., *Image rights of sportsmen in Russia as institute of private law*, in Modern Law, N. 12, 2013 (in Russian). (Е. А. Вострикова, Р. Э. Полухина, *Имиджевые права спортсменов в России как институт частного права*// Современное право, N 12, 2013).

UEFA Supporter Liaison Officer Handbook (2011 edition), http://www.sdeurope.eu/resource/uefa-official-slo-handbook-2011-edition-eng/

Zaitzev U. V., *Legal nature of the transfer of sportsmen* in Sport, economics, law and management, 2009 (in Russian). (Зайцев Ю. В., *Правовая природа переходов спортсмена* // Спорт: экономика, право, управление, 2009).

Selected Bibliography

Zaitzev U. V., *Peculiarities of termination of labour contract with sportsmen*, Materials of the *II* International Conference on *Sports law: perspectives of development* (in Russian). (Зайцев Ю. В., *Особенности прекращения трудового договора спортсмена*, материалы *II* международной научно-практической конференции *Спортивное право: перспективы развития*, М. 2008).

Index

The numbers here refer to paragraph numbers.

Index

www.ingramcontent.com/pod-product-compliance
Lightning Source LLC
LaVergne TN
LVHW021108300926
849160LV00009B/653